D1633729

# POSITIVE
# NOT PUSHY

**The New Learning Centre**

Skills for Success at School and Harmony in the Home

**211 Sumatra Road, London  NW6 1PF**
**Tel: 020 7794 0321   Fax: 020 7431 8600**
**admin@tnlc.info   www.tnlc.info**

Director: Noël Janis-Norton

*By the same author*

How To Be A Better Parent

# POSITIVE NOT PUSHY

## How to make the most of your child's potential

Cassandra Jardine

**Vermilion**
LONDON

For my invariably positive mother

1 3 5 7 9 10 8 6 4 2

Copyright © 2005 Cassandra Jardine

First published in 2005 by Vermilion,
an imprint of Ebury Press, Random House,
20 Vauxhall Bridge Road, London SW1V 2SA
www.randomhouse.co.uk

Random House Australia (Pty) Limited
20 Alfred Street, Milsons Point, Sydney,
New South Wales 2061, Australia

Random House New Zealand Limited
18 Poland Road, Glenfield,
Auckland 10, New Zealand

Random House South Africa (Pty) Limited
Endulini, 5A Jubilee Road,
Parktown 2193, South Africa

The Random House Group Limited Reg. No. 954009

Papers used by Vermilion are natural, recyclable products made from wood grown in
sustainable forests.

Typeset by SX Composing DTP, Rayleigh, Essex
Printed and bound by
Mackays of Chatham plc, Chatham, Kent

A CIP catalogue record for this book
is available from the British Library

ISBN 0-09-190020-4

# ACKNOWLEDGEMENTS

In addition to all those quoted in this book, I should like to thank the many other children, parents, teachers and coaches who gave me the benefit of their experience. There are too many to mention every one by name, but my special thanks go to Tania Heyworth (and all her friends), Kate Sabisky, Carla Rapoport, Clare Reynolds, Victoria Broackes, Claire Geber, Keith and Charlotte Browning, Laura Jane Goffin, Jane Wroe Wright, Brett Moore, Polly Samson, Alexandra Campbell, Roger and Eden Silva, Maria Leach, Oenone Williams, Christina Hughes-Onslow, Ros Badger, Fiona Tong, Cathy Wearing, Anthea Rowan and Chris Drew. I am grateful, too, to all those who helped me at GB Tennis Girls, the Football Association and many other organisations.

Of course, I should also like to thank my own family: William, Oliver, Eliza, Dido, Christabel and George for putting up with my experiments in being positive not pushy. And all those who teach my children the various things they are learning outside school: Pav, Tim, Russell, Maritza, Faye, Michelle, Austine, Angela and all the rest – thank you for doing such a brilliant job.

I am grateful, too, to Yanis Maillaris for setting up my website and Christine Boyd for the use of her photograph.

# CONTENTS

# INTRODUCTION

We all want the best for our children,
but nobody wants to be a pushy parent.
How do you achieve the one without becoming the other?
On behalf of my five children and their sanity
I decided to find out.

The pushy parent is one of the unequivocally demonic figures of our time. We all love to sneer when one of them makes an appearance on television or in the press. With glittering eyes and set jaw, trophy-laden mantelpieces and drawers full of rejection slips, such parents are frightening to others who are keen for their children to do well. No doubt they are even more terrifying to the children who bear the brunt of their ambitions.

The pushy monster of legend not only sends a child to a hot-house school that will ensure precocious achievement by over-loading the child's evenings with homework, but he or she also expects a child to excel in all kinds of other ways too. 'My child the tennis champion', 'My son the chess grandmaster', 'My daughter the violin prodigy': such phrases roll around the pushy parent's head while the wretched mite is locked into a practice room or tennis court.

When someone else's child achieves something young – not necessarily international fame, but perhaps Grade 5 in piano by the age of eight, or a walk-on appearance at the Royal Opera House – other parents tend to look straight past the child's triumph to the shadowy Svengali whom we know must be lurking just behind. 'My child may not know how to serve at tennis,' we tell ourselves, 'but at least she is happy and normal – and I am not such a pathetic loser than I have to live through her successes.'

Any envy we might feel of the other child's achievements is swiftly diverted into gloating anticipation of the human car crash to come when the poor brat finally wises up to the intolerable pressure he is under. Like actor Macaulay Culkin and violinist Vanessa Mae, mathematician Ruth Lawrence or tennis player Mary Pearce, the child is eventually expected to put as much distance as possible between himself and the hard parental taskmaster.

Deep down, however, I don't feel comfortable with this smug assumption of superiority based on 'normal' children's lack of achievement – not least because I know that I could often be accused of being a pushy parent myself. On the morning before I wrote this I had a salutary moment when I was caught out going over the top.

I had been putting one of my children forward for sports scholarships to secondary schools because she loves football, swimming, gymnastics and tennis. Of course, I also thought that some money off the fees would be no bad thing. I wasn't expecting her to get a scholarship, but she was keen to try and I wanted to help her, so I had asked her various coaches for letters in support of her attempt. The previous week, one of them had obligingly showed me the rough draft of her letter. It mentioned my daughter's reliability and positive attitude to being taught but, having read it, I asked, in what I thought was a mild manner, 'Do you think you could say something about her showing promise? The school will, after all, be hoping that a sporty child will win competitions for them.' Then I left.

It was my husband who went to collect the letter from the woman, and he came back convulsed with laughter. 'She was very embarrassed,' he said. 'She told me that you had asked her to put down that the child was a champion and she didn't feel she could. And,' he couldn't resist adding, 'you are the one writing a book about pushy parents.'

When I stopped cringing I could see what had gone wrong. In my embarrassment, I had put a request too vaguely and had in the process come across as hopelessly unrealistic about my daughter's talents. What made the incident all the more galling was that it was far from the first time I had managed to come across as hideously pushy – even though I don't really care a jot about whether any of my children win medals or turn out to be a world-beater.

The catalogue of similarly embarrassing moments is long. There was the time when one of my daughters came back in tears from her new secondary school because she had not been picked for a part in a play. 'I am the only one in the whole year who auditioned for it and wasn't given anything, not even a part in the crowd,' she wailed. After a wearing evening, I picked up the phone to the drama teacher the next day to say how upset my child had been to be singled out for humiliation. Very gently she informed me – as I should perhaps have guessed – that my daughter was far from the only one who had not been given a part and that, no, the drama teacher would not ask her to help out with props as a consolation prize because the GCSE class had that job.

I could go on and on. I have pressed teachers to put children in for musical grades before they are ready. When doing so, I have excused myself by thinking that it would be nice for the child to feel she has moved up a stage, though, in truth, I suspect it has mattered more to me than to the child. I have also put my children up for tests that they were bound to fail – entry to a special language class was one such.

At least I haven't been as unkind as some parents. At one school meeting a head teacher begged parents not to put their children in for high-ability tests if they had no hope of passing. The previous year, she said, some children had barely been able to write their names and had spent the two hours of the test sitting doing nothing. But I have often bought my children educational toys, such as Lego sets and jigsaws, aimed at much older age groups because I fondly believe that my little, ahem, prodigies must surely be capable of doing them. Invariably, I have ended up doing the jigsaw or constructing the pirate ship myself with the child by my elbow looking bored.

I have also thrust my children towards all manner of activities simply because they are available. 'When I was a child,' I think, 'I would have loved to trampoline or sail, therefore they must.' And when one of my children has shown the mildest interest in anything – chess or bridge, skating or cricket – I have set up or sought out classes to further their nascent interest. Often this has simply had the effect of snuffing out the initial spark.

At times my children have been so overloaded with extra-curricular activities that they have been staggering from one to the next. 'She looks tired,' I remember someone observing caustically of my hollow-eyed daughter. When I counted up I discovered that the child in question had no fewer than 15 scheduled after-school and weekend engagements: ballet, tap, singing, tennis, football, French, piano, chess, drama, pottery, art, Brownies, skating, Kumon maths, swimming . . . It was enough to cause a mental breakdown, had the child not sensibly asked to drop some of them.

I have managed to turn one of my children off all organised activity, apparently for life, by sending him off on endless weeks of mixed sports every holiday. The poor boy was miserable because he likes just to drift around and hates crowds. But I thought it was a good idea, so I would resort to bribery, prise his fingers off the car door, register the reluctant soul and run. Each time I was probably as unhappy as he was for the rest of the day.

Why have I been so pushy? Of course, like every parent, I think I am acting in a child's best interests. Despite the standard view of the pushy parent, I don't think I am driven by a desire for reflected glory – though I wouldn't mind some. My main reason for sometimes driving my children too hard is curiosity.

When I was little so much less was available for children. My parents' view of an all-rounder was of someone who could do both maths and English, not diving and violin, rugby and canoeing, skiing and cookery, art and astronomy too. They let me try a few things, but they were glad when I gave up because my parents' generation did not expect to fit their lives around their children's schedules, as we do now.

Working women like myself seem to have fuelled the boom in extra-curricular activities. Mothers who are at home at teatime didn't feel, as many workers do, that if they can't always be there, they can at least spend their earnings on giving children an interesting life. Activities assuage parental guilt: if a child is out doing something, I tell myself, she isn't just flopping in front of the television or vegetating because I am not around to stimulate her with games and conversation.

These days we also know more about the benefits of all kinds of activities, from playing Mozart to an unborn baby to learning a language at an early age. (Failure to do the latter means that unused brain pathways will close down by the time children are grown up, so they may have forever missed the boat for learning a second language.) And, of course, this is a more competitive world, with open-ended expectations for each child. Doctors' children still often become doctors, but there is no longer the assumption that a child will take over the family business, run the farm or go down the mine because that is what has always happened.

If we are to give children a wide choice of future occupations and pleasures, we need to nurture their talents, so, like many of my contemporaries, I am always on the lookout for the next bright idea on offer. Children seem to have boundless energy, I often feel, as I shoo them into the car at dawn. How much better to expend that energy on swimming lessons and football rather than trashing the sitting room or messing up the garden.

What I forget is that these activities require not only physical exertion, but mental energy too. It was only when I started to follow the lead I was setting my children and embarked on tennis lessons to improve my low-level game that I realised that even the most pleasurable activities are stressful. I love my tennis lessons, but I am also acutely conscious of not doing as well as I would like, of letting partners down, of infuriating the coach or thinking someone else is his favourite.

As adults we tend to stick to doing whatever we are good at, the activities in which we have some expertise. As soon as I tried to improve my tennis, I found myself instantly standing in a child's shoes. For children, everything they learn is new, everything they try they have to get better at. It is hard mustering the enthusiasm to keep going when you feel a flop; agony fighting back the tears when you get it all wrong. It is equally tempting to brag when something goes right, and then to feel fearful of not being able to repeat the success.

Despite those insights, my struggle to improve at tennis did not make me want to stop pushing my children into new activities, but to learn how to motivate them better. I have loved the fresh air, the company, the exercise and the feeling that I am getting better at something, however slowly. It has made me wish that I had become competent in more fields as a child and been more assiduous in trying to learn more skills in later life. When I felt discouraged I saw, as an adult, how shockingly easy it is to give up on a challenge; how much easier, then, for a child who has not yet learnt perseverance.

I didn't wish to stop being pushy, I decided, if pushy means introducing my children to all kinds of new interests. Nor did I want to follow the advice of one pregnant friend who found my mania for activities baffling: 'Surely it is better just to let children play with a stick in the back garden,' she said. I don't believe she became as accomplished as she is by pushing a stick around, and I wonder whether, when her baby has grown up a bit, she will continue to take such a laid-back line.

In my experience, children – if given endless blank time to fill – do not always find their own interests. It takes a parent to find out that judo happens on Wednesday afternoons, a parent to get the child to the lesson and a parent to pay for the course and buy the kit. Those parents I know who can't be bothered to do this have children who sit around all day watching television or playing computer games. They aren't learning to use their imaginations – they are preparing for life as couch potatoes – and the only skill they are acquiring is the ability to use a console or a remote control, which might be useful if they were intent on becoming fighter pilots, but not for much else.

But the anti-pushing ethos is in the ascendancy these days. We worry terribly that children's imaginations are being stunted. Anything to do with making a child undertake something that isn't 100 per cent fun, or the child's own idea, is often thought cruel. A father I know, who has only a very young child, explained to me that he intended to prevent her doing all the activities on offer. 'She will be allowed to follow a passion if she has one (so long as it isn't ballet, which I detest),' he said, 'but I don't want her learning anything mechanically. It must come from the heart.'

Unfortunately, there are very few passions that children will discover for themselves. Football, electric guitar, skateboarding are about the extent of it. Apart from those, children are naturally slobs. Without some parental pressure, they will hang around all day in their pyjamas, just as they scoff crisps and fizzy drinks in preference to eating fruit and drinking water. They may sometimes try things on impulse if they have seen someone else doing them, but as soon as the going gets hard or the weather becomes less than perfect, they give up. Unless, that is, they have a parent who is prepared to make something happen.

Despite the current concern about children's stress levels, those that I see are very rarely over-organised. Some schools do give out too much homework to children too young, just so they can develop a temporary edge to justify the school fees. I also find that there is a stage towards the end of primary school when children seem to want to try too many new things because they are eager for new challenges. But most children still seem to have enormous stretches of down time.

However many improving activities I line up for my children, they still seem to know the lyrics to the latest Britney Spears song, to know every episode of *Little Britain* by heart and to have more than enough time to chat to their friends on the Internet. Yet, although many parents are prepared to give children the chance to try some of the myriad activities on offer these days, we are scared of being thought pushy if we expect them to put much time or effort into them in order to become any good. So when a child kicks up a fuss about his tennis lesson, I let him off, and when a child seems determined to make violin practice a misery, I let it drop.

I am buying temporary peace but possibly at the expense of their future happiness. They need interests to take them out of themselves. When William Hague was booted out of the leadership of the Conservative party it was playing the piano that cheered him up. And hasn't many a marriage been saved because a husband plays Sunday football or a wife can bash out her frustrations on the tennis court?

A few years ago I noticed that life in my home was not as calm and orderly as I felt it should be. There was no obvious problem, no child with a behavioural disorder who caused disruption, just the ordinary friction arising from children who don't always want to do as they are told because it doesn't suit them. It was then that I started going to parenting classes and realised that if I wanted a better atmosphere at home, I was going to have to abandon the comfortable notion that I could be a cosy friend to my children. I needed to become a parent in charge – which didn't mean becoming an old-style martinet.

The techniques I was taught by two parenting advisers – Noël Janis-Norton and Luke Scott – had a magic effect on all the flashpoints, from bedtimes to car journeys. The atmosphere at home changed, became more positive and less full of screeches and wails. But once I had cracked the major causes of strife at home, I began to wonder what else I had not been doing as well as I might have done. It did not take me long to work out that I needed to put more effort into helping my children succeed.

Before then, apart from occasional anxieties about being too pushy, I had thought I was doing well by the children simply because I was spending every weekend – and most of our disposable income – taking them from one activity to the next. What I found, as I watched them try one thing after another, was not that I regretted giving them all these tasters – I certainly wasted a good deal of money, but it did no harm. Far from feeling I had put too much pressure on them, in fact, I felt that I hadn't been effective in my attempts to broaden their interests.

The five of them – two boys and three girls aged from fifteen to six – have tried all sorts of things, but when they were very young I now see that I hadn't done sufficient research to sort out the best options from the plethora of alternatives, bearing in mind their temperaments, ages and stages of development. Nor had I worked out how to help children stick at things and develop the habit of self-motivation.

I had also let the children use their busy-ness as an excuse for bad behaviour. I found, for example, that I could be held to ransom by the investment I had made in a term's dance tuition. When the child made a fuss I would fork out for new kit, regardless of whether I thought she needed it, just to keep her going.

Observing other parents, I found the ones I admired were not those who had taken the 'play with a stick in the garden' line, but those who had been more effectively pushy. Their children seemed to have learnt what fun it is to commit to something and, in some cases, really excel at it. These parents were not monsters with wan, exhausted children who talked precociously of their admiration for Descartes. Their children seemed delightfully bright and bouncy, confident and positive. They seemed to have learnt the lesson that my children's swimming coach keeps repeating: 'Don't kill time, spend it.' What had these parents done, I wanted to know, to get such good results?

Often these parents were not pushing a child to excel, but taking charge and making it possible for the child to do far better than anyone ever thought possible. I came to see the so-called pushy parent as heroic in many ways. He or she gives up time to ferry children around, to watch and encourage them in their activities. He invests in their talents. This might mean spending just a few pounds on tuition, or, for some dedicated parents, it can mean selling the house and moving to be near the National Ice Centre in Nottingham or a stage school in Surrey. Most of us are *not* prepared to do that for our children, but are we right to condemn those who do? Is that so much worse than buying a house within the catchment area of a good school? Is Suzuki violin good, but are flashcards bad?

When Scarlett Johansson took to the stage after she won an Oscar and a Bafta for her performance in *Lost in Translation*, the first thing she did was to thank her mother for taking her to auditions and buying her hot dogs afterwards. The talent is Scarlett's, but she wouldn't have been able to make use of it without a dedicated parent. Nor could any of the sporting stars, from Tiger Woods to Serena and Venus Williams, have got where they have without fathers (with sports it often seems to be fathers) who ferried them around and kept their spirits up when the going got tough. After several years of winning tournaments, the Williams sisters have now said that they would like to relax more and study art, piano and languages. But that doesn't mean that their father, Richard, was wrong to help them get where they have.

Occasionally, someone, such as rugby star Jonny Wilkinson, excels without appearing to be the product of pushiness (though he has, of course, a mother who drove him to matches and training sessions). We can then applaud their achievements with a clear conscience. But even when there does seem to have been considerable parental pressure, it often seems worth it to the successful. I doubt if Kiri te Kanawa regrets her international singing career, or Vanessa Mae wishes she had never picked up the violin, even though at times both have found their mothers overbearing.

But before I got carried away with enthusiasm for learning how to be the right kind of pushy parent, I suffered qualms of self-doubt, so I rang the British Psychological Society and asked for the names of psychologists who had worked on the subject. I was told of two experts in the field and rang them in trepidation, expecting them to consider me wrong-headed for even asking if there was anything to be said for pushiness. What they had to say surprised me.

The first psychologist I spoke to was Dr Jack Boyle, who has studied gifted children. I asked if he believed the pushy parent of today was either a myth or rightfully condemned. 'Most parents will deny it, but most of them are pushy,' he replied. There was a pause, and I quailed in anticipation of a lecture about children's need to relax more and have more time to discover their own creativity, but he continued: 'It's a good thing, of course. Children have to be taught that success doesn't come on a plate, that to succeed you have to go through the pain barrier, and to accept rejection.

'We've lost this understanding of the pain barrier today, but you need to go through it to be an artist or writer or musician. The middle classes like to pretend that their children's achievements are effortless – "He's so bright, he just sailed through . . ." they say, but that's not good for the children. In my field – psychology – the vast majority don't finish their PhDs, not because the task is too difficult, but because a PhD is not something you can just get from the petrol station along with a sandwich and a can of Coke.'

I then spoke to Dr Ruth Coppard, another child psychologist, again expecting to be given the let-them-just-play line. Again I was amazed. 'Parents aren't pushy enough,' she said without hesitation. 'I was thinking recently about Queen Elizabeth I and how many languages she spoke at a young age. Today, by contrast, there's a general inertia. With one child you are pretty busy, and with more than one there's a lot to do, but it is also because we put so much energy into children's academic achievements that we don't give them wide enough opportunities.

'For example, we all desperately want our children to read by the time they are six, but reading is a physically linked capability, something that parents can't do much about. A second language, however, is something children can do best when they are very young. We could talk to our toddlers in other languages, yet most of us don't. Nor do we tend to think that developing physical skills is particularly worthwhile.

'Periodically,' she said, 'I feel guilty that my own son didn't learn a musical instrument. He wanted to play the trumpet, but wasn't allowed to until he got his adult teeth. By that time he had gone off the idea.' If anything, she concluded, she wished she had been pushier with her children when they were young.

Those conversations were a tonic, but not one that made me feel much better. They made me realise that although I was pushing children to try all sorts of things and offering them all the opportunities and trainers that money could buy, I wasn't actually very well informed about how to do the job well.

My approach was haphazard. I hadn't thought much about what children could manage at what age or how best to introduce them to new skills and experiences. Nor, in view of the constant protests and tears over violin practice or tennis lessons, had I worked out how to make them want to do their best. Also, when a child developed a passion for something, such as gymnastics or the guitar, I hadn't worked out how to keep the child from becoming obsessed. Nor how to help that child develop other skills too, ones that she might not embrace with equal enthusiasm. In short, if I was going to be a pushy parent I wanted to be better at it. That became the quest that led to this book.

## About this book

My focus is on the activities that children do out of school. This is partly because I have already dealt with many of the issues surrounding school in *How to Be a Better Parent*: these include getting children through the classroom door in a positive state of mind, making sure the homework is done on time and to a decent standard without dramas, handling bullying and developing good relationships with teachers.

Undoubtedly, academic results are the area in which most parents are tempted to push, justifying themselves by thinking that they are doing so for the child's future. Those parents may forget all the wider interests that a child might develop. Or they may approach them with the same zeal as they do academic success, and thus risk alienating the child from both the activity and themselves.

In relation to school, pushy parents can make a nuisance of themselves by being excessively anxious and critical, both of children and of teachers. They can be unrealistic about their children's abilities, controlling or needlessly competitive. Alternatively, they can learn to be positive, supportive and motivating. All these issues are seen at their starkest in out-of-school activities.

With extra-curricular areas parents have a freer rein either to enrich their children's lives or to make them a misery. Outside school, parents are on their own in their attempts to help children develop a wider range of talents than a school, with its limited time and resources, can provide within the constraints of the National Curriculum. Parents can either use their own time and efforts to widen their children's experience of all life has to offer, or they can seek out expert teachers and coaches to do the job for them.

Since we are either doing the teaching or paying for it, we feel the anxieties related to these activities more keenly. The issues of how to motivate a child and how to help him deal with success and failure are down to us. If a child shows a flair for something, it is the parents who have to decide how far to go, whether to let it become a huge part of a child's life – indeed, of the whole family's – and to be clear about the effects this may have on the child's behaviour

## The research

In search of useful advice about how to develop children's talents without making them unhappy, I turned to various sources of wisdom. The first was other parents whose children seemed to be doing well at all manner of things. Their children were not necessarily showing exceptional talent – though some were remarkable by any standards – but they were persevering and improving. Such parents had sensible, practical advice to pass on as a result of their triumphs and mistakes.

Then I spoke to children about what they found helpful and

enjoyable, and what they disliked. I also tracked down adults who had been successful as children to ask what had helped them become achievers and about the long-term effects of success.

But I wanted more than the guidance of those who had only personal experiences to offer. In search of a wider understanding of the issues and of general solutions to common dilemmas, I turned to the parenting experts whose advice on behavioural issues I had found so inspiring that I had felt impelled to write a book about it, *How to Be a Better Parent*. I felt sure they could help me see beyond the immediate problems to the underlying issues related to achievement.

Noël Janis-Norton, who runs the New Learning Centre (see page 190), jumped at the chance to pass on the advice she has given to many parents through her work as a teacher and parenting expert. 'The first thing parents ask me – once they have tackled their children's behavioural problems – is how they can help them do well,' she said. As a mother of two and a foster parent, she has encouraged her own children to develop their talents. She has also, in the course of a thirty-year career, thought long and hard about the question of how to help a range of children make the most of their talents or, as she puts it, become 'all they can be'.

Over the years, Noël has known children who have been involved in many different fields of sporting and artistic achievement. She has advised parents on dilemmas relating to children who are succeeding and to those who are not. She has counselled parents who are pushy in the worst sense of the word and those who have been too passive and need to learn how to help their children become more successful and self-reliant.

Coming from a family of musical and artistic prodigies (she herself was considered artistically gifted as a child), Noël knows what parents can do to encourage children's talents without making them feel under excessive pressure. Some members of her family have made the most of their gifts; others have not. Some found their gifts more of a burden than a source of pleasure and would even have wished to be more ordinary. 'It all comes down to parental management,' she said. 'The key lies in the sixteen skills.'

Those skills, which I learnt to use and then described in *How to Be a Better Parent*, range from 'being in charge' and 'presenting a united front' to 'setting rewards and consequences' and 'providing children with a healthy lifestyle'. Those skills are implicit in much of the advice that Noël – and others – impart in this book, but there are two skills that require more detailed explanation because they will keep coming up in later chapters.

The first of these is descriptive praise. This is emphatically *not* the kind of praise that involves giving children a big round of applause for their feeblest efforts. Praise of the 'super', 'marvellous', 'aren't you clever!' variety is evaluative and, in Noël's view, both demotivating and ineffective as a way of making children feel confident. A far better kind of praise, which she teaches parents, is descriptive praise. This focuses not on the achievement but on what the child is doing that you wish him or her to do again or build upon. It is not an exclamation, nor overblown, but a statement of fact as in: 'I like the way you have got your violin out even though you don't feel like practising,' or 'I'm glad that you have come out to play football on such a wet day.'

The other key skill that I found I needed to employ frequently in my attempts to help the children make more of themselves was reflective listening. This doesn't involve asking a question such as, 'How did it go today?' and listening to the answer (if you get one). It involves having the courage to imagine what the child may be feeling but dare not articulate for a range of reasons, which might include embarrassment at admitting failure or fear of a parent being cross. 'Maybe you are feeling disappointed because you really wanted to be in the A-team but weren't picked' would be an example of reflective listening if a child is refusing to go to a match. Another might be: 'It must be very frustrating feeling that you tried so hard but lost. I expect you think you never want to play again.' This kind of listening doesn't involve solving problems, but helping a child work through feelings so that he can find his own solutions.

Luke Scott, the other parenting adviser whose wisdom I once again sought out, subscribes to Noël Janis-Norton's sixteen skills. However, his perspective on the questions for which I was seeking answers in this book is different. As a dyslexic whose exam results were not what they might have been, he dropped out and became a waiter. It was only several years later that he began to work with troubled young people and, from that, became a parenting adviser, specialising in difficulties with boys.

His approach is, predictably, laid back. 'Parents want to teach their children to succeed,' he says. 'But what is success? Surely it is not a simple matter of exam results but something far wider, about self-motivation, commitment and study skills.'

In addition, I also wanted specific information related to different sports and arts. For that I spoke to coaches and teachers in many different disciplines, each of which is included in the activities section at the end of the book.

**Note:** The text refers equally to 'he' and 'she' because the issues covered are not gender specific.

# 1

# THE WRONG KINDS OF PUSHINESS

Why do well-intentioned parents become pushy?
What are the anxieties that drive pushy parents?
How can I stop myself being pushy?
What does it feel like to be pushed?

Most parents are pushy. We may not all cram our children with culture, but we want our children to do well and we imagine that what we are doing will help them. We repeat precocious remarks, horde snatches of praise to share with relatives, stick their certificates on the wall. We love it when a child does something well – and so we should. Children thrive on approval and encouragement. We want them to try the next thing. We want them to do as well as they can. When does that become harmful?

The parents I spoke to who provide their children with masses of support and encouragement know that others consider them pushy. They don't like the word, but they are prepared to live with the sneers because they believe they are doing the right thing by their children. They know that behind every child who succeeds is a parent who has driven them around, foregone weekend trips and holidays to attend rehearsals or matches, insisted that homework and practice are done, and spent large sums of money to give the child a chance to try new things or pursue a passion.

They say that the charge of pushiness is one levelled by lazier parents, and is one that envious parents fall back on when their own child is doing less well than someone else's – often because they haven't put in the effort to motivate their own child. 'Too few parents push their children,' said Ken Rose when his son, Justin, won an open golf tournament. 'Too many allow them to make their own decisions, and most times when kids make their own way they get it wrong.'

One mother who has made considerable sacrifices to let two of her children pursue their interest in dance says: 'Children can't look to the future in the way adults can. A lot of the behaviour that some people see as pushy is a way of frantically fighting the child's corner.'

Perhaps in that word 'frantically' lies the pivotal point at which some parents overstep the mark from encouraging and supporting into pushing and putting too much pressure on children. I asked Noël what she thought. 'All parents think they are doing their best for their children,' she replied, 'even when they are misguided. There's a fine distinction between pushing and being supportive or encouraging, and parents may not know when they have crossed it. Calling them "pushy" makes it sound as if they don't care about the child, when in fact they care desperately.'

She is frequently consulted by parents who are worried about a child's behaviour or lack of motivation. Often, she finds, the parents have unwittingly driven the child into a state of misery or rebellion. To help them find a better way of relating to the child she finds it helps to identify exactly what it is they are doing, as a wide range of behaviour is lumped together in the word 'pushy'.

She starts by unpicking the word 'pressure', which can also have many different meanings. 'Often it just means expectation. Yes, there is an expectation that you will do five ballet lessons a week because ballet is not something you should practise much at home, as it can lead to bad habits of posture and technique. It would be wrong to view that as pressure: it is simply what is required.

'Sometimes when a child talks about pressure she means that the parent or coach will be upset or disapproving if she gets it wrong. For example, when a child says, "My dad puts so much

2

pressure on me about sport," it usually means that the father is in the habit of giving negative feedback about the child's level of skill or willingness to practise.

'The important thing is to work out in each case what the parents are doing wrong. That way they can correct themselves. Usually the problem is one of poor communication as a result of some underlying anxiety.'

Even the pushiest parents can be helped to reform, she believes, since what they are doing is well intentioned. 'I have seen pushy parents transformed. There are moments of lucidity when they wonder if they are doing the right thing. If, then, their child – or someone else – gives them feedback in an unmistakable way, the parents will question themselves.'

## The critical parent

This is the most common sort of pushiness, in Noël's view. 'Parents don't realise they are being critical. They think they are giving advice or constructive criticism, but it comes across as negative. So long as parents remain positive, they are supporting rather than pushing their child, and it will do the child no harm. But when a parent starts criticising a child for not winning or not trying hard enough, it can be bad for the parent/child relationship and bad for the child's self-esteem.

'Often such parents don't realise they are being negative,' she says. 'They say, "Keep your eye on the ball", which is positive, but they say it again and again – and they say it when the child has just missed a shot. So even though the words are not, "You stupid idiot, why did you . . . ?", the effect is negative.'

A tennis coach told me that when a girl is having problems on court it is usually because of issues off court. One girl who used to get very nervous before matches admitted that this was because her father was watching. He could be so critical. When the coach told the father, he was amazed; he had no idea of the anxiety he was generating.

Parents who want to be involved, says Noël, should put their efforts into giving positive talk-throughs in advance to prepare children for what is about to happen. 'That changes the atmosphere from negative to positive. For example, if a parent said before the match, "Keep your eye on the ball", it would be neutral. And if the parent said afterwards, "And that time you did keep your eye on the ball", it would be positive. Enthusiasm with positive feedback isn't pushy.

'Often parents are critical and unable to share the child's enjoyment in an activity because they are disappointed by the results. The child then feels his best effort is never good enough. If, instead, the parent focuses on giving positive feedback through descriptive praise of all the things the child has done well, the child still knows that the parents feel he is very talented and has a responsibility to go as far as they can with the talent, but it doesn't feel like pressure.'

## The protective parent

'This kind of pushy parent doesn't necessarily want the child to be best at something. She hopes that a particular activity will make him more confident, and assumes that by doing well he will come to feel better about himself,' says Noël. 'When the child doesn't then do well and doesn't seem more confident, the parent becomes critical of the coach and the organisation. Even if the child is successful, he may not become as confident as the parent hoped, so again the parent can be difficult and defensive on the child's behalf.'

Noël believes that parents who worry about confidence may not have much confidence themselves, so she helps them to explore their own feelings. 'If, for example, a parent wants a child to carry on with the piano, even though he is plainly hating it, it might be worth asking the parent to reflect on how her life would be different if she had carried on with the piano herself. People always think that if they had been encouraged to develop their talent as far as it would take them, they would be happier and more confident.

'I help people to see that no single activity is the reason why someone is unhappy or not confident,' she says. 'Confidence comes from feeling competent at all kinds of small things, from learning to enjoy doing your best (which you can do at any age), and from feeling that approval doesn't depend on performance.'

Noël remembers a child who arrived at a violin lesson having not practised, and was told by the teacher that she wouldn't, therefore, be able to learn a more difficult piece. 'The mother knocked on the door to explain why she hadn't practised. The teacher said, "It doesn't matter why; the consequence is that she has to do the easier piece." The mother was quite unreasonably upset and the teacher branded her "pushy".'

Protective parents are often labelled 'pushy' because they want their child to be given special treatment – either because they have so much talent or because they are so sensitive that they would be terribly upset if criticised for, say, not arriving on time. In doing so, the child is being protected from experiencing the consequences of his own actions, which is not a good idea.

## The impatient parent

Luke Scott feels that impatience is another reason why parents can appear pushy. 'Such parents can't wait for results to come in their own good time. They always have to be hurrying the child onwards and upwards.'

Increasingly, childhood is viewed as a sprint, but children who are subjected to unreasonable pressure to achieve fast suffer from stress and burn-out.

'The impatient parent,' he continues, 'gets so het up about children doing well that he forces the pace and leaves the child feeling that she is never doing quite well enough.'

The solution lies in making the parent realise that although there may be a small window of opportunity for winning Wimbledon, most activities don't work like that. Indeed, the child who achieves very young because of intensive coaching may fall behind when others catch up.

## The rushed parent

This parent makes even enjoyable activities into something a child dreads by always working against the clock. 'Even if a child is enjoying an activity,' says Noël, 'he may want to stop because he can't bear the hurrying. The child feels everyone is constantly annoyed with him, and he can't do much about it. All he ever hears is, "Hurry up", "We're late", "Let's go" and "Don't dawdle".'

The problem may be due to over-scheduling the child, or not thinking ahead and getting things ready the night before. But it can also be a habit of mind that the parent has got into. Those parents, she believes, should learn to handle time better or else prune their schedules. The children will be far happier relieved of the rush, even if they would like to carry on with the activities.

'People talk about time pressure,' she says, 'as though it is not their choice how they fill their day. It is anxiety-inducing to feel you are not accomplishing things as well as you would like because you are so busy, and for many parents rushing about feeling anxious is an illness or addiction. They are so busy thinking about all the other things they have to do that they find themselves thinking about work when they are at home, or thinking about the children when at work, or thinking about the shopping when playing with the children.

'If parents want to keep to a tight schedule, they must take the burden of keeping an eye on the clock themselves, and shouldn't transmit their anxiety to the children by nagging.'

## The unrealistic parent

Ballet is a field in which parents are often considered monsters of pushiness, but Lucille Bryants, who runs the London Children's Ballet, believes that 'there is no such thing as a pushy parent, only an unrealistic one'.

Often when parents beg and bully Bryants to cast their little prodigy in a role she finds she can solve the problem quite easily:

'I ask them to watch some of the other children auditioning. Soon they realise that their child is not as outstanding as they had hoped, and may not even be as good as the rest of the class. Once they know, they tend to behave rather better.'

There are two kinds of lack of realism, Noël finds. Some parents, like the ballet mothers above, are unrealistic about the current levels of a child's talents. Other are unrealistic about the level a child might eventually reach. When the child isn't doing as well as expected the unrealistic parent blames the teacher or the organisation for not serving the child well, although the real problem is lack of talent.

To make parents more realistic she asks them to start noticing what the child is actually doing rather than focusing on the stage they would like the child to be at. It is also wise not only to talk to coaches and teachers about the child's level and potential, but also (and this is the hard part) to listen to their answers without extracting just the little bits of information that you would like to hear.

## Parents who want their child to be the best

When children feel their best is not good enough, they become defiant and stop trying. Noël had a pupil who was an amazing ice-skater, a high-flier at her club. The child was winning trophies, but was proving difficult at home, so one day Noël reflectively listened to her. 'It must make you feel good that your parents are so proud of you,' she said, and the girl replied: 'Well, no, because they are always wanting me to be the best and I'm not always the best.'

Parents who want their children to be the best get angry with them when they make mistakes and the children then lose confidence. The skater's parents hadn't noticed they were doing this. They had started the child on skating because she had poor coordination, and they thought it would give her confidence. When she started excelling at skating they had become over-excited on her behalf. 'The most important thing is the enjoyment,' Noël reminded them.

When the light dawned they said to their daughter: 'Of course we want you to keep skating, but we won't love you less if you are not the best.'

## The frustrated achiever

The standard explanation given for the parent who is a little too eager for a child to do well is that he or she is a frustrated achiever. So behind every ballerina is a failed dancer with bowed legs, and behind every star golfer is a father who took up the sport too late to excel.

Noël finds this is often the case. 'The parents may want children to succeed either because they didn't have the chance themselves,' she says, 'or because they did have the chance and weren't the best.'

Such parents can get carried away and may not be sympathetic to a child who has all the advantages that they lacked, but doesn't deliver. They can be highly critical, and a child with a sensitive temperament can find it intolerable to have to achieve not only for himself but also for his parents.

Noël taught two sisters who were both members of a skiing team. 'The father had been a competitive skier who had left the field,' she says. 'He was incredibly keen on his daughters winning. He would say he wasn't, but you only had to read his body language and his distress when they were injured and couldn't compete. On one shocking occasion when one of his daughters was injured he didn't seem to be thinking about the fact that she was in agony as muscle had been ripped from bone, only about completing the season. He sounds heartless, but he only ever wanted the best for his children. He thought winning would make them happy.'

The girls had very different temperaments and responded to the pressure accordingly. One got so anxious that she suffered from irritable bowel syndrome. The other didn't absorb her father's anxiety. She was motivated to do her best, but her father still felt she wasn't trying hard enough because she wasn't reaching the standard he wanted.'

## *The ambitious parent*

Ambitious parents, rather than protecting children from the achievement culture, thrust them into it. They may even resort to cruelty to achieve their ambitions: the footballer Peter Shilton has said that he was made to hang from the banisters while his mother tried to stretch his legs. They may even justify the pain by saying that children who have had rough treatment are extra motivated because they want to dish out the same level of torture to opponents.

This type of parent sees a child's talent as the passport to a better life, not only for the child, but often for the whole family. With the large sums of money available in many fields these days, that it understandable. A child can earn £25,000 from a single television commercial – enough to buy the whole family several good holidays. Naturally, parents take their child out of school for such work, believing that it is in their best interests – which it may not be long term.

The pushiest parents tend to be found in sports where there is big prize money because there is a tangible reason to win rather than just to play the game. So football and tennis have become the focus of parental ambitions in a way that judo and cricket have not.

Of course, if parents were to study the odds on a child making big money, they might think otherwise. Those in the lower echelons of the tennis world top 100 are probably making barely enough to pay their coaching costs and travelling expenses, while even chess grand masters tend to be poverty-stricken.

Sometimes the ambition may be social rather than financial. Those who run riding schools often find that parents are keen for their children to ride because it is a pastime of the rich crowd, whose social acceptance they crave, even if the child would rather kick a proletarian football around. One riding instructor told me how she saw crying children being pushed into the ring by their parents. 'A lot of it,' she finds, 'is because parents have missed out as children themselves because they couldn't afford it.'

## The narrow-minded parent

This parent is a cultural snob who will support a child, but only if he or she wants to do whatever the parent thinks suitable. So piano lessons are fine, but not tuition on the electric guitar. Ballet is acceptable, but not for boys. Girls are expected to steer clear of the contact sports that might damage their looks. The narrow-minded parent leaves children with a limited view of what kind of success is acceptable – a stifling attitude that leads spirited children to rebel.

Noël herself had a mother who, like most people, had a narrow definition of creativity. Playing a musical instrument would have been OK, although the family never stayed in any place long enough for her daughters to learn one. Art and poetry were also acceptable. 'It didn't occur to her or to me,' Noël says, 'that there were many other ways to be creative, and it was only as an adult that I found teaching was my way of self-expression.'

The experience has led her to arrive at a wider definition of a creative talent: 'Your talent is the thing that, whenever you are doing it, all your cares go away. Musicians and actors say there comes a point when you don't think of all the preparation – the music or words just seem to flow through you. I get that from teaching.'

## The single-minded parent

When a child shows ability at something that does meet with parental approval, there can be a tendency to over-focus on that one activity, rather than find ways to develop the child as a rounded personality. A parent can seem pushy when he insists on a child sticking to something at which he has shown some ability; invariably with younger children it would be better for them to have more variety.

Tennis players, for example, need to develop their general fitness because tennis is a single direction sport that uses one hand more than the other. At least until the age of twelve, their tennis, as well as their general well-being, would benefit from another sport too. Even children with artistic or musical talents need physical exercise, which can sometimes be forgotten.

Single-minded parents may be unaware that a child becomes stale doing too much of one thing, and will develop better if given more variety. A father who signalled his ambitions by buying his nine-year-old son golden golf clubs found that the child soon refused to play the game because he felt it was being shoved down his throat.

The very single-minded often educate their child at home so that enough time can be devoted to the one activity. The child's social life can then depend too much on those whom he meets at the activity – and that can increase the sense of competition and anxiety levels.

## The self-sacrificial parent

This parent has given up a lot for a child to pursue a dream – which may have been the parent's dream to start with – and expects something in return. If a child is not delivering, the parent is unhappy and makes the child feel guilty. Guilt always leads to resentment.

Such parents have to remember that it was their choice to invest so much time and money in the child's talents. The child could have been told 'No' or made to settle for something similar but less demanding – perhaps in-line skating as opposed to ice-skating – that does not require hours of driving and getting up early for practices.

## The ignorant parent

This parent is a bane in the lives of many teachers and coaches because he knows rather less than he thinks he does about both psychology and the rules of the activity. He sees a foul where there was none, and challenges the linesman. The ignorant parent is seemingly unaware that causing embarrassment is not going to enhance a child's performance. Many tennis clubs have had to ban parents from sitting beside the courts because they won't accept a call of 'out' against their child's serve.

A little knowledge is a good antidote to too much emotion. It can make such a difference to the atmosphere among football supporters that the Football Association has established a kite mark of quality for those amateur clubs in which the parents have gone through their Internet-based 'soccer parent' courses and, presumably, emerged the better for it. 'We won't stop them standing on the sidelines,' says an FA executive, 'but we can ask them to count to 100 before they shout at the officials or the players.'

## The anxious parent

Anxious parents are always fretting that their child would be doing better, going further, if the teacher were more sympathetic, if the child were in a different group, if the club were better run, or if the school had a different ethos. Luke Scott describes this kind of parent as 'worrying that everything will go wrong and that the child's life will be awful unless she gets to the right university, which means the right secondary school and even the right nursery'.

His antidote to that is to remind parents that people develop at different rates. 'Some of my school contemporaries had discovered their passions by the age of fourteen,' he tells them, 'but many others, myself included, had not.'

'Often this kind of parent is insecure,' says Lori Ferguson, an educational psychologist who worked for the National Association for Gifted Children. '"Am I doing enough?" they worry. "If I don't do more, will the giftedness go away?" A parent who was gifted and given no encouragement often wants to give the child everything. She sees a spark and bombards it, then the child doesn't have the opportunity to say, "I've done it and I don't like it." My advice is to slow down and to provide the child with opportunities and encouragement more gradually. The child doesn't need everything now.'

'Anxious parents need to look at themselves,' says Noël. 'They don't see the world as a safe place. If they didn't have a child with a talent to worry about, the anxiety would come out in another way.'

## The victim

'Another characteristic of pushy parents,' says Noël, 'is that they feel like victims. If a child is late or hasn't got the right kit they will harbour a grudge against the teacher who dares to criticise. They are ready, willing and able to register all signs of irritation as slights, and if a child doesn't get a starring role, to imagine that it is because teachers and other parents have plotted against this child. Those parents are competitive and stroppy, full of jealousies. Often such parents would like their child to be more motivated. When they aren't, they resent those whose children are.'

Those who feel like victims can either look at people – or say things – in an aggressive way. That puts the teacher's back up, makes the child embarrassed and gets the parent a reputation for being pushy.

## The parent who wants a child to be grown up

These parents can't accept that the child acts, thinks and talks like a child. They can't, for example, let a child answer a question in an immature, blithery way. Rather than let the childishness be apparent, these parents interrupt and answer the question for the child. They are always trying to fix and make better, and won't let the child be at whatever stage she has reached.

## The boastful parent

The boaster never fails to mention her child's achievements, even if there are others in the room who are doing at least as well. This parent also has a tendency to encourage the child to whip out his violin at any gathering, to the annoyance of other adults who may not want the child to dominate. Children of such parents can appear over-confident because they have been encouraged to show off. Underlying the child's behaviour may be a fear that the parent will no longer love him if he is not the centre of attention.

Often the truth is more than the parent can bear. Not long ago I read a sad story about a child who played the violin at two and chess at three. Aged four, he was enrolled on a computer maths course at Stanford University, but at the age of seven he started screaming in a Harry Potter film, and he now suffers from suicidal tendencies. His mother later admitted to having faked some of his results.

## The controlling parent

This parent wants to be in charge of the child's progress and tuition. He breathes down the necks of coaches, and sits in on as many matches and practice sessions as he can, even if he is an unwelcome distraction. He may become the child's manager, trapping the child in his control.

Sometimes controlling parents lose perspective to such a degree that they harm their children in what they believe to be their best interests. Child star Judy Garland was signed by MGM at the age of thirteen, and her contract stipulated that if her physical appearance changed so that she could not perform satisfactorily, she could be suspended without pay. Her mother put her on drugs to control her weight, starting a long-term addiction problem.

## The over-stimulating parent

This parent has been described by actress and mother of two Jane Horrocks: 'These parents buy the latest child development fad, thinking they can give themselves "excellent parent" points.' It becomes a vicious circle. The organised child is less able to organise himself.

'It may be a symptom of older parenthood,' she says, 'the wish to keep children so busy that parents only have to put them to bed exhausted. I was shocked to discover that some of my son's schoolmates had schedules so hectic that their parents carried appointment diaries for them.'

'Why does everything have to be for a purpose?' complained my fourteen-year-old once when I suggested he stop watching TV.

## The competitor

Competitive parents want a child to do well, but only so long as she does not beat them. Of course, if the child is any good at whatever it is the parent is promoting, by the time she is in her mid-teens, the child should be able to beat the parent.

The parent who won't be beaten is unwilling to accept that he is growing older, and also won't allow his child to grow up. While most parents like being beaten by their children and can enjoy the child's victory as cheering confirmation that their child is a success, some parents feel a sense of loss when victory is no longer theirs. Children of such parents often grow up to fear success.

## The unconfident parent

Parents who are nervous of pressurising their children often make their children's lives harder by not being clear about what is required. Day-to-day life soon becomes a struggle, and the parent has a choice between taking charge or letting the child give up.

Noël gives the example of two sets of parents who both told their children that they were to do music until a certain age. 'One set was very positive and there were no grumbles,' she says. 'The other pair made a big issue of explaining and then arguing and negotiating. Those parents felt they had to persuade their children, that it wasn't the parent's right to say what was to happen.

'Imagine,' Noël told the latter pair, 'if you negotiated each day with your child about going to school.' Of course, they could see it would be unworkable. 'We assume school is very important, so we don't negotiate about it,' she says, 'but we may not be so sure of the value of extra-curricular activities. From the beginning you have to be clear in your own mind. Is it up to the parent to decide? Or the child? Or to the child who throws a fit? Or to the child, but only after a three months trial? You must decide who decides. When you do it, it is a relief all round.'

## What does it feel like to be pushed?

I spoke to a young musician, brought up in Russia, whose parents were determined that she follow them into a musical career. 'Both my parents were professional musicians, so I didn't have much choice,' she says. 'I was locked in a room practising my instruments for several hours a day throughout my childhood.

'Music in Russia is a part of the culture, and also a way out of the country. Both those factors made it easier to work hard and enjoy playing. But my parents could be quite critical, especially if they didn't think something was perfect. I felt pressure to succeed as far as they had, if not further. They were great, but I still feel nervous performing in front of them. The Russian mentality is that you mustn't give up, you must never say, "This is it". It's not a competitive spirit so much as a compulsion to keep on growing.'

As a child, she was exceptional and travelled Europe winning many competitions. The travel was exciting and it also meant that, to her great relief, her parents were less involved in her daily professional life – 'their pressure took a back seat' – because she was often away. Aged fourteen, she won a scholarship to study at a prestigious music school in Britain.

'The danger of achieving so young,' she says, 'is that you get put on a pedestal too soon. Loads of the pupils at special music schools (such as Chetham's, the Menuhin or the Purcell) found it really tough when they went on to the Royal Academy or Royal College of Music and suddenly found that they were not unique any more, got no special praise and had to live in digs. Many left college after a year. One or two have become big stars, but four or five of those in my year won't have anything to do with music any more; they won't even play for pleasure.

'My parents were thrilled when I won a scholarship to Britain to study, and I have only recently realised what a sacrifice it was for my mother to send me away. But now I find it hard talking to them. They ask, "Why aren't you with this or that orchestra?" They would like me to be a soloist on a high chair. I normally tell them that I am doing what I can, that I put in the hours of practice, but for the moment I am a freelance musician and still, at twenty-four, trying to get into an orchestra.

'I have rebelled – more inside than outwardly. My younger brother is more musical than I am, but because the family have emigrated from Russia there are more possibilities and he's much lazier than I am. He quickly worked out that you could make a better living as a banker or accountant.

'I love what I do, but I did lose control of my youth. It would have been interesting to see what else I could do. Music does, however, bring amazing highs. I love playing and bringing pleasure to people.

'If I have children, I shall introduce them to music, but I wouldn't lock them in a room. You can get far without working quite so hard when you are young. And when they are older I would tell them exactly what kind of a life it is as a musician.'

# 2

# THE POSITIVE PARENT

How much can I teach my children myself?
When does the time come to get an expert to teach?
How do I choose a coach? How can I carry on helping a child?

Often children think they can do things just because they have watched other people doing them. 'Oh, that's easy,' they say, seeing Jonny Wilkinson score a goal in rugby – until they try it. As they get older, inertia and self-consciousness make it harder for them to try new things, unless they are in the habit of having a go. A recent survey of 11–20-year-olds found that more than three-quarters of the girls and two-thirds of the boys said they would like to be fitter and take more exercise, yet the desire alone had not been enough to get them off their sofas.

It is down to parents to get children up and running since, left to themselves, most children will do pretty little, especially if there are the attractions of television and computers to absorb them. If they do try something, they are unlikely to push themselves to become really good at it, unless it is something socially cool, such as rapping. So the initiative has to come from parents. They have to introduce children to good ideas, just as they have to put the right food in front of them if they want children to eat the requisite five portions of fruit and vegetables a day.

Parents have to make decisions, take charge and follow through if they don't want a child's experience of music to be limited to MTV, and for games to mean zapping inanimate foes on a screen. Luke Scott's mother used to tell him, 'Most people only find what they are good at by trying lots of things. There is always something that you are better at than other people.'

'Many famous and successful people have a parent – usually the father – who is determined to help them do well,' he says, citing the Williams sisters, whose father set out to make them champions from birth, and Beyoncé Knowles, whose father formed a pop group for her when she was twelve. 'Is that good or bad? Who's to say? What is clear is that people are good at things because of their parents.

'There are far more second-generation footballers in the best teams, for example, than would get there by mere coincidence. Even taking into account an inherited aptitude, the chances of two people of such talent coming from one family is very small.'

There is so much that parents can do to help their children make the most of themselves that the choice is bewildering. Some say that we use only 1 per cent of our brain capacity, others say 10 per cent – either way there is plenty of scope for activating unused parts of children's brains while they are young enough to learn fast. Often the best place to start is by playing with them, finding out what they enjoy and building on that – without getting too hung up on whether they are going to be wonderful at something.

## Why children need to do things

Extra-curricular activities are helpful for a vast range of reasons, including the following:

**Antidote to self-obsession.** Most girls become obsessed with their looks if they haven't found another way to express themselves through a talent or a skill that boosts their self-esteem.

**Confidence.** The child who learns from drama lessons to stand up and speak in front of an audience may never hold an audience at the National Theatre enthralled, but he will find it a lot less stressful to give a presentation, be interviewed or even conduct a telephone call.

**Fitness.** The benefits of exercise include a better immune system, stronger bones and less body fat. Teenagers who do a sport regularly are less likely to suffer from depression or to go for chemically-induced highs than those who don't.

**Letting off steam.** Boys in particular can be rowdy and even destructive if their energies aren't channelled.

**Maturity.** Outside school and away from home children feel they are treated more like responsible adults, so they learn to behave in a more mature way.

**Relaxation.** The teenager who, when life gets tough, can sit down at the piano and play something, maybe a piece that they learnt long ago, is less likely to suffer from stress.

**Role models.** Children, especially older ones, need adults other than their parents to look up to. Teachers and coaches whom they see outside school may be just the job.

**Self-discipline.** Knowing what it takes to become good at something is invaluable. Noël's aunt, a concert harpist, used to say that performing is the best antidote to self-indulgence. 'Once the red light is on,' she would say, 'you're on.' Under the spotlight you can't dither or make excuses.

**Self-reliance.** In activities outside school, children have to take charge of themselves, to accept responsibility for their own success and failure.

**Social ease.** Activities outside school introduce children to a wider range of children. Lucille Bryants, who runs the London Children's Ballet, loves listening to children from varied backgrounds meeting each other. 'Ballet,' she says, 'is generally considered a middle-class activity, but it has far wider appeal. I hear children with drivers waiting to take them home being told, "You're posh" by others. Often it is the first time the privileged children have thought about their good fortune.'

**Team spirit.** Working with others teaches cooperation. A show-off child who takes part in a performance can learn that she is only a small cog in the machine.

**Understanding.** The child who has learnt a musical instrument or studied dance will be a far more involved and discerning member of an audience.

## Where does a parent start?

Noël finds that most children can become good enough at something to enjoy it and can develop character-building skills without needing to have any outstanding natural talents. To get them started they need a parent who is in charge. 'Even though a parent is not infallible, he or she has more experience, maturity and wisdom than the child,' she says. 'Therefore, the parent needs to be in charge.'

She defines being in charge as:

- Becoming clear about what your goal is and why it is important to you.
- Knowing what you want to have happen.
- Learning how to make it happen.
- Doing what it takes to make it happen and carrying on doing it.
- Avoiding whatever will have the opposite effect.

She favours exposing children to lots of activities, with the teaching, as far as possible, integrated into family life. 'Most parents have so many skills they could pass on to their children,' she says. 'Parents can do a lot of what they pay experts to do. If they can, it is better for both the child and the adult because doing things together builds relationships. Time is more important than skill.'

Paul Gold, a tennis coach who has a small child told me that he is not going to send him off to lessons with anyone else for quite a while. 'People often ask me, "Can you give my three-year-old a lesson?" My reply is that it is a waste of money as the child will miss too many shots. Instead, I tell parents to play games with their child in the garden or the park to help them develop the coordination that will help them with all games later.

'With little ones, concentrate on running, jumping and balance. Can they run backwards? Can they coordinate their arms and legs when they are running? Teaching them these skills is like programming a computer for when you want to use it later. Teach them posture by simple tricks, such as getting them to draw their belly button in to their spine and pull their shoulders back.'

Ex-tennis champion Shirley Brashier believes that parents are their children's best coaches (she coached her own children to high levels): 'You have the same genes – not just the good ones, but the bad ones too – which people sometimes forget.'

---

**THE SKILLS NEEDED FOR SUCCESS**
Parents can teach and train children all the essential skills below, says Noël:
- Following instructions immediately.
- Accepting and learning from correction.
- Practising until you can do something automatically and well.
- Keeping going.
- Thinking about solutions, not about problems.
- Not bending the rules or expecting others to bend them for you.
- Paying attention to detail.
- Learning from mistakes.
- Being friendly and polite (even when upset).
- Leading a sensible lifestyle (healthy food, enough sleep).
- Accepting and giving praise.

---

## How to help children yourself

The obvious advantage of being your child's teacher is that there is less hassle and expense. More subtly, you also incorporate the activity into normal life, which means that it is more likely to become a part of the child's life.

So cookery courses are all very well – though, in my

experience, the children only learn to make disgusting pizzas and fancy biscuits – but teaching a child how to make a meal for the family by doing it together is better. With the latter, in due course, you can expect a child to cook unsupervised, whereas the only long-term benefit of the cookery courses I have paid for has been the apron I bought as a souvenir.

If a child doesn't find something easy, a parent is often better placed than a coach to spot whether the child has the necessary building blocks – what Noël calls the 'microskills' – in place to be able to do it. A child cannot, for example, draw unless he can hold a pencil, or get ready for football if he can't tie laces.

Although it sometimes doesn't seem like it, the more a parent is involved in doing something with a child, the keener the child will be. I have found there are often grumbles and power struggles while the activity is taking place, but that afterwards the child is eager to repeat on his own whatever we were doing together.

## How to get better at teaching your own children

Noël views many parental attempts to help children as too half-hearted to be effective. For example, if the child shows an interest in something we buy them books and software to give them a boost. Then, after a quick glance, those books and DVDs sit on the shelf unused because children can't motivate themselves. 'It takes an adult's enthusiasm and a structured approach to get them started.'

The most educational toy is not the one pitched at an age above your children's. Far from 'stretching' them, it often leaves them frustrated and defiant; the most educational toy is an interested adult.

The mistake I tend to repeat as my children's teacher is to make the session, whether of tennis or maths, overlong and too elaborate. 'I don't want a complete numeracy lesson,' groans a child with whom I am playing times tables games.

Noël's advice is always to keep it simple and short so that

the child is left wanting more, rather than dreading the next marathon session. And never keep the child waiting for hours before you start because you just have to put the washing on. If you say you are going to go swimming at 5.30, then you have to stick to it.

I have also learnt from experience to adapt activities so that they are within a child's grasp. Success should be easy to achieve, so a narrow goal with the child as shooter is a mistake, as is putting the basketball net at adult height. Similarly, some children can grasp the bidding system at bridge, but many find it easier just to play out the hands, as in whist, with the trumps already decided. Using all the chess pieces from the beginning is confusing for a child, so most professional teachers start with just a few and work up to the full set.

Another way to keep a child interested in learning a game is to vary the rules. Instead of playing to win, you could occasionally make the object of the game to lose as many card tricks as possible.

---

**USEFUL GAME-PLAYING SKILLS**
Parents can teach children the following useful skills:
- Keeping an eye on the game, even when you don't have the bat or ball.
- Moving forward to catch or hit things.
- Running without knocking into anyone else.
- Noticing boundaries, such as flower beds.
- Following instructions, e.g. run forwards, run backwards, turn round – as in 'Simon Says'.
- Sticking to the rules.

---

## Why don't parents teach their own children?

We are too busy, too scared of getting it wrong, too keen on the latest fashionable class that other local children are attending, too keen to show that we are lavishing all the riches of the world upon our children in the mistaken belief that they will think that is better proof of love than spending time with them.

I am as guilty as the next person of sending my children out to classes in things that I know I could teach them myself. When Noël chided me for it, I protested, 'But it takes up too much time.' 'So does driving children around,' she replied.

One mother who used to take her unwilling child to a dance and drama class looks back on it with regret. 'Why did I bother?' she has asked herself. 'Why didn't I just put on some music at home?' Her answer is: 'I wasn't thinking so much about the child as about having a bit of peace and quiet myself so I could get on with what I wanted to do.' In retrospect, it wasn't worth it because she spent much of the time worrying about whether the child was happy and dealing with his dread of the next lesson.

My children have often complained about being sent to formal classes when they would rather play at home. It is too late for me now to replace Tumble Tots with home gym, and I doubt if I would ever have the patience of tennis champion Steffi Graf's father, who would throw balls to her when she was tiny for four hours at a time. Nor can I aspire to the image of the Victorian family all playing and singing together around the piano – at least not until one of the children makes up for my own deficiencies at the instrument.

But I can play charades to develop their acting skills, devise singing games for car journeys, be an enthusiastic audience for their shows, and stand in goal. Making Christmas decorations at home is muckier than sending the children off to an art and crafts class, but it is a lot cheaper.

Pianos and keyboards are fun just to play around with when a child is too young to take lessons. Despite having backed out of my own piano lessons at an elementary level because practising clashed with playtime, I know enough to help a child pick out a simple tune. It can't do much harm if a child simply bashes around a bit, making noises: one of my children has taught himself to make quite coherent noises, just by ear.

My chess is very basic but it is good enough to satisfy my younger children. Even I can throw a ball straight enough to amuse my six-year-old. If I dared, I could also bicycle with them to school.

## Why do parents give up teaching their own children?

It isn't always easy being your own child's coach. It requires forbearance and a willingness to accept that the relationship has to be more formal than at other times. A tae kwon-do champion who was taught by his father says: 'My coach is my dad. That can be hard. If your coach tells you to do something, you just do it, but if your dad tells you, you tend to answer back.'

Over the years that boy has learnt to respect the difference between his father as coach and his father as dad, and 'just got on with it'. But many find it too much of a strain.

Spence Curtis, the father of Jade, a promising young British tennis player, told his daughter to call him 'Coach' when they were training and 'Dad' at home. She soon got tired of trying to make that differential, and called him rude names, such as 'Git', at home to make the point. He now formalises their professional relationship by fining her if she is late or disorganised.

Observing other parent–child relationships in which the parent is also the coach, he believes that when they have soured it is usually because of a control issue. 'With a parent as coach you can have a lot of success. You can put the athlete first, but you have to work through problems.'

In Noël's view the relationship works only if the parent is capable of being consistent and controlled. If he is sometimes firm and sometimes lenient, the relationship quickly becomes open to manipulation.

'Unless the parent is consistent, the child won't take him

seriously, and a coach *has* to be taken seriously. Any parent who becomes a coach – or, indeed, a home educator of any kind – has to think through the rewards and consequences that apply if a child does or does not do as required.

'Children are very sharp at spotting when a parent isn't firm, so the parent has to be clear in his own mind whether something is required or optional. He also has to be prepared to stand firm when a child whinges.

'The problem is usually the level of emotion involved. Children are testing all the time – all the more reason for a parent not to give in and allow a child power that she shouldn't have.'

## What makes a child a desirable member of a club or team?

The list put out by the Football Association of what they are looking for in a young footballer is not what parents might expect. There is no mention of talent or inspiration; instead, they say a child needs: a good attitude, sportsmanship, to turn up on time, to shake hands with opponents, to wear the correct kit (but no jewellery), to have clean boots, not to eat, chew, swear or fight, or make abusive remarks, on or off the pitch, and to respect the manager or coach. 'Remember, football is only part of your child's life,' the FA exhorts parents. 'Offer only positive encouragement, help at the club, lead by example, let the coaches coach, let the children play.'

In many activities, good behaviour is often more in demand than brilliance. A casting agent told me that when a child is picked for a role in a show she is, of course, concerned that the child looks and sounds right and can do whatever is required, but there are usually several such candidates. The one she wants is the child who passes a different kind of test. Does he turn up on time? Is he reliable (you don't want a child absent at the first sniff of a cold)? Does the child get enough sleep? Will the parent pick up punctually? She asks drama teachers only to put forward such candidates.

## HOW PARENTS CAN HELP CHILDREN TO BE GOOD PARTICIPANTS

- Train a child not to complain. My local Stagecoach organiser finds that in every lesson the same children keep coming up and saying that something is wrong with them. 'You can tell when a child is really ill and the ones who keep coming up for attention,' she says.
- Teach a child to ask, not demand.
- Recognise that just because a child has a passion or a talent doesn't mean she can do as she pleases.
- Just because you approve of an activity doesn't mean it should become a way for the child to learn to manipulate adults. When my daughter was behaving badly one day, she gave a forthcoming gymnastic display as an excuse, saying she knew I cared about it too. 'I care far more about your behaviour,' I told her. She looked taken aback.
- Keep up a routine.
- Remember who is in charge.
- Judge a child by his social competence, not by his ability at chess or violin.
- Give detailed feedback, not just on the child's performance, but on his behaviour.
- Create the circumstances. A mother who wanted her sons to sing, but didn't want them to feel self-conscious, deliberately sent them to a single sex school.
- Give them good examples to follow. And avoid the bad ones. A father who takes his children to their modelling assignments said that they are much better behaved than the adult models as 'they don't bitch about one another or pick at food and worry about their figures.' Contact with such adults is one reason to be wary of putting children in for modelling.

## Can a parent teach an older child?

As children get older, we tend to think that the parental teaching role is finished and that they need expert tuition. Noël doesn't believe it is always so. 'When my son was twelve,' she says, 'I taught him to read music and to play simple tunes on the recorder and piano.

'I didn't know how to myself, but I wanted him to enjoy making music. We house-sat for a month in a place with a piano. I got some second-hand piano books and we worked through them together. It was a terrific bonding experience for us at an age when kids are moving away from their parents and thinking them uncool. It showed him that adults can keep learning (they tend to see only adults who are already good at things) and that I too enjoyed learning. He also learnt folk songs, which he wouldn't have otherwise.

'The only benefit he didn't get was being taught by an expert. And that's the least important thing.'

With the help of books and guides, a parent can keep one lesson ahead for quite a while. Even with drawing, something for which I have never had an aptitude, there are wonderful books around that show you how to structure a landscape, or how the different bits of the body fit together, using the simple and effective method of copying.

There's nothing wrong with copying. That's how we learn to do most things, and copying should not be confused with cheating. Tracing cartoon characters is a good way for a child to learn about pencil control. These pictures may not be admired by art teachers, but they give a child the confidence to experiment on her own afterwards.

But there will still come a time when it seems sensible to hand over to someone with more expert knowledge. In ball games, for example, some skills are innate – pace, balance, coordination – and some are so general that a parent can teach them. Technical skills, however, such as how to serve like Roger Federer, can only be learnt from experts. Without expert tuition a child will have to reinvent the wheel, or he might develop bad habits that will be hard to shift later (I still find it hard to face sideways rather than forward when hitting a tennis ball). So there comes a time when the most helpful thing parents can do is to accept that children need someone else to teach them. Then you have to search for a coach.

## How do you choose a coach?

Choose carefully. It may sound obvious, but many parents are far more trusting of those they send their children to outside school than they are of schools and those who work in them. There is a tendency to pick the nearest class and assume it will be all right because the teacher has the relevant qualifications. We shove the child through the door and bolt, when it would be better to watch a class before signing on, to see if the teacher has energy and humour – and makes constructive corrections.

A coach might not want a parent to sit in on a lesson, but he should see it as a reasonable request. Some are even grateful for it. One football coach, who has suffered from ambitious parents, says that he wishes they had found out before they sent their children to him that he takes a non-competitive approach.

I have been caught out many times by sending my children off to grumpy or lazy coaches who seemed charming at first. I only rumbled one swimming teacher when I swam alongside a lesson – not my children's – and heard her making sarcastic remarks to a fat boy who kept doing belly flops. And I hadn't noticed, until one of my children grassed on him, that the cricket coach was turning his back on the lesson to practise his golf swing.

It is not sufficient to ask a teacher what his or her lessons are like. 'Even if the teacher is honest,' Noël says, 'he may be unable to articulate how he teaches, or the approach he takes. A lot of sports coaches think that it is part of the job to loosen up "spoilt" middle-class children, so they go in for a lot of coarseness. It's no good finding out halfway through the year that the teacher makes dirty jokes; if you are going to be upset, it is better to know sooner rather than later.'

## What am I looking for in a coach?

A coach is an expert in a particular sport; someone able to train a child in good habits so that she doesn't develop bad ones or injure herself. The best teacher may not be – indeed, often isn't – the most talented performer at a particular activity. Stars often find it tiresome having to teach for bread and butter money when they would rather be performing or playing themselves, so they may be impatient with less than perfect pupils. 'Great chess players can't bear telling a six-year-old how to move pawns,' says Bilal Ghafoor, who was never good enough himself at chess to compete at a high level, but loves teaching. 'I don't get irritated when children make simple mistakes.'

'The problem with many dance and art teachers,' Noël says from long experience, 'is that they have what is called an artistic temperament. They are intense and impulsive, whereas teachers need to be calm.' Similarly, many sports coaches can be too macho. They shout and order children about like sergeant majors, and, as former or frustrated players themselves, can be too focused on winning.

Also, Noël points out that people tend to become teachers because they are good at something. 'The particular skill has come to them so easily that they don't understand why it doesn't to others. Those teachers are not much good for beginners or those who don't catch on fast.' She believes herself, for example, to be a very effective maths teacher precisely because, as a child, she struggled to understand mathematical concepts, so she knows what the problems are and how to explain them.

'A good coach or teacher will not judge,' she continues, 'but will encourage the child to develop his own judgement so that he can realise when he has done as well as he can and where he has made mistakes. He will also discourage children from becoming too big-headed and dwelling exclusively on their past successes rather than on where they have to go next.

'Children need to learn from adults who show they are worth respecting, who allow them to make mistakes and learn from them, who simplify the complexities of life by establishing clear expectations.'

According to Noël, coaches and teachers need:

- To know their field and (even more importantly)
- To know how children learn.
- To know how to motivate. This includes being firm with both parents and children about showing up, bringing kit, respecting rules and practising.
- To set a good example.
- To explain clearly by breaking down the activity or skill into little bits and showing the connections. Often teachers can do whatever it is intuitively, but demonstrating is not enough. The child may think the teacher is showing off and feel that she can never be as good, so what's the point in trying.
- To be available to parents.
- To be clear and consistent about what is expected of children and parents, and what the sanctions are if they don't match up. (English people often sound tentative when they don't mean to.)
- To have a philosophy, an approach.
- To understand crowd control.
- To be enthusiastic.
- To have a long fuse, self-control and composure.

Of course, no coach or teacher will have all these strengths – they are only human. A parent needs to know what the weaknesses are in order to work around them. If, for example, the coach is disorganised, you know that you must double-check when half-term is and what equipment the child needs to bring next week, etc.

## Parental help behind the scenes

There are various unintrusive ways that parents can offer children support.

**Boost water intake.** A recent survey showed that half of

parents think seven-year-olds need only three glasses of water a day, not quite half the amount recommended by nutritionists. As a rule of thumb, for each kilo of body weight one should consume 30ml of water. Children are prone to dehydration because they have a greater surface area to volume ratio than adults.

The odd thing about thirst is that children cannot always recognise it in the way they do hunger, so parents have to keep reminding children to drink. Often, in fact, a child will get muddled and say she is hungry and eat something when thirst is the real problem. When swimming, it doesn't occur to children that they could be thirsty.

Water is essential to well-being and performance. It increases the ability of the blood to carry oxygen to the brain, thus improving concentration. A mere 2 per cent loss in body fluids can cause a 20 per cent drop in physical and mental performance. Coaches therefore encourage children to drink before they feel thirsty – by the time they register thirst, their performance has already dropped. Water flavoured with a little grape or apple juice is supposedly most effective in persuading children to drink more.

**Ensure good nutrition.** As manager of Arsenal, Arsène Wenger has paid great attention to the players' diets. One of his favourite sayings is: 'If you eat a sticky toffee pudding, you play like one.'

Everyone needs a balanced diet, but sports nutritionists say that children doing stop-start sports, such as cricket or tennis, have a particular need for carbohydrates that give instant access to energy and so parents should keep up the fruit and vegetables.

Those who take part in endurance events, such as marathon running, have to be careful to consume fats that will provide slow-release energy over a longer period of time.

The brain consumes a disproportionate amount of the body's energy, and parents may underestimate the effect of concentrating hard. Chess players often lose 6 kilos during a tournament – not because they are so engrossed that they forget to eat, but because they are thinking so hard.

**Provide plenty of layers.** Children aren't good at regulating their own temperature. They often find themselves too hot or cold because they don't anticipate the weather by looking out of the window. Parents frequently cosset their children by telling them what to put on and take off, and sometimes even traipse around in their wake loaded up with alternative garments. It is better for children to learn to control their own temperature, and certainly to carry their own belongings. Send them off for activities with lots of different layers to shed or put on. Of course, you run the risk of losing unmarked clothes but that is better than a child who loses interest in football purely because he felt cold one morning.

**Reduce screen time.** Children who often complain of being too busy to do all kinds of things, from sports to homework, nonetheless manage to fit in ten or even twenty hours' viewing a week. Once in front of the screen, it can be hard to get away, as the rays both overstimulate the brain and inhibit children from moving off and taking action.

Research recently suggested that reducing a child's viewing time by seven hours a week would reduce the risk of obesity by 30 per cent. In those seven hours a child can take a lot of exercise and learn many more useful skills than dexterity with a remote control.

**Set reasonable bedtimes.** Of course, parents should make sure children get enough sleep. (For tips on bedtime issues see *How to be a Better Parent.*)

---

**THE POSITIVE PARENT SHOULD . . .**
- Make sure to get to lessons on time. Many kids, who would never be late for school, are always five minutes late for extra-curricular activities. This never goes down well, and it embarrasses the child. Collecting on time is equally important.

---

- Don't let anything interfere with the lessons. extra-curricular activities are as important as going to school. Every term my children complain about having to go to Saturday afternoon drama when there are other things they want to do. I have set a rule that they are allowed to miss one lesson per term, but once they have used that option up, there are no further exceptions.
- Make sure the child has the right equipment and that it is washed from one week to the next.
- Fill in the relevant forms and leave a message if the child is not well.
- Talk about the activity in between times so that the child knows what you expect of him and has the opportunity to discuss any worries.
- Be there for matches, concerts and shows.
- Pay subscriptions and fees on time.
- Accept the drudgery. A parent's role involves washing kit, helping with administration, promoting events and activities, ferrying and chaperoning other people's children.
- Promote fair play by setting a good example.
- Support and encourage if the child has had a bad day.
- Take a child to watch competitions.
- Talk constructively about other players and performers.
- Respect the coach's private life and do not contact him unnecessarily.
- Show appreciation of the coach's efforts, and only discuss concerns about training or matches with the team manager in private.

## Does the positive parent have to be a martyr?

I have met very little resentment among those parents who put a lot of time into getting their children going on activities, or supporting them as they move on to higher levels of an activity. Often they are giving up most of their free time and large sums of money to help a child. One tennis father was typical when he told me that he never minds a minute of the time he spends driving his daughter around and watching her play. 'Often I am moved to tears watching her, by seeing a little girl so involved,' he says.

Another woman, whose every weekend for half the year is spent taking her children to ballet rehearsals, has come to love that time, not just because she is sharing something with her children, but because she gets to meet all the other parents who have made the same sacrifices. 'One mother with a talented child who wanted to audition pulled the child out when she heard she would have to give up her weekends. Other children have whole families or grannies who spend all day waiting to take them home, often long distances. Their devotion is incredible.'

My own findings since I have started actively encouraging my children's activities is that I have widened my own rather narrow interests as a result. I have loved watching sports (however cold it can get) and listening to musical instruments being played. Moreover, seeing what pleasure the children have derived from these activities has got me off my backside. It took two years of children's swimming lessons for me to pluck up the courage to ask the coach for some advice on my own strokes. I find I can now skate myself, having eventually tried it. As for tennis: in order to be able to play against my children as they get older, I have been taking regular lessons myself. I will never be very good, but that doesn't matter. I feel fitter and I love it, despite moments of despair.

Much though parents may groan about it, ferrying children from one activity to the next is not just a curse of modern life – and the just desert of the pushy – it can be a delight. Time alone in a car provides a wonderful chance to get to know a child, to discuss what is going on in her life, administer some descriptive praise and listen reflectively to her feelings.

The hard part for parents is doing all those things to support a child without becoming more involved in the activity than the child himself.

**WHAT'S NOT PUSHY?**
- Letting children know what you admire and value. 'My parents didn't push me,' my godson told me. 'They subtly poisoned my mind against the things they didn't want me to do.'
- Talking to a child about the point of games.
- Sharing your own enthusiasms, but with a light touch (keep visits to galleries and concert halls brief).
- Broadening a child into a well-rounded human being.
- Asking about results and celebrating successes.

# 3

## THE WELL-ROUNDED CHILD

How do I choose an activity for a child?
Will trying new things give a child confidence?
How far should I let a child decide?
How do I say 'No' to a child?
What is the best age to start something?

Choosing the right activities for a child is a more complex process than it might at first appear. At its most basic, the choice might be determined by what the child wants. Unfortunately, this may bear no relation to what the child needs. Decisions can't be left to a child's whim because he or she will have no idea of what is on offer, or what won't be available at school.

In fact, so much is on offer, especially if you live in a major city, that it can be bewildering – not just to you, but also for your child if you were to sign him up for even a small fraction of it. Then, within any one subject, such as music, there is a variety of approaches and a wide choice of instruments to consider.

Narrowing down a choice depends on knowing your child and what might suit and benefit him. It also depends on knowing what you are realistically going to be able to manage logistically and financially.

The choices available fall into three broad categories – sports, games and arts. Schools can take children only a limited distance with these because they don't have the time or the resources. Parents can do much more for their children out of school, which will stand them in good stead for later life.

These days the only sporting activity that many adults indulge in is a trip to the gym; more frequently, they fork out for gym membership but rarely use it. Gyms aren't the answer for children. Most gyms won't even admit children, and standing on a treadmill or pumping away at a rowing machine is lonely and dreary – as many adults find. My dog won't run unless there is some good reason, such as a ball or another dog to chase, and children also need an objective.

Sports foster team spirit and competition, self-reliance and cooperation. Those who have done sport regularly from an early age talk fondly of the sense of belonging, the excitement of achievement. They also say that if an injury prevents them carrying on with their favourite sport, they take up another one rather than become a couch potato. The habit of sport is one that stays with you for life.

The same goes for the arts. A child who develops a love of ballet may not go on to be a ballerina – few do. It's a hard life, and parents often want to steer children away from it, but it takes only a small shift for the child to move on to salsa or some other kind of dance. The chances are that with some ballet training the child will do well at any dance form.

In adult life there may be few opportunities for playing a trumpet, but the knowledge of music that a child has acquired will make it far easier to transfer to the piano or an instrument that can be played in a rock band. Games such as chess or bridge, or skills such as conjuring or puppetry, will never desert a child and will be something that he can use, in due course, to entertain his own children.

But there is also another category of choice that many parents tend to overlook in favour of more showy activities: the domestic arts. Knowing how to cook is a relatively rare skill in an age when new flats for twenty-somethings are often designed with only a fridge, kettle and microwave, but no hob or oven because it is assumed that young professionals don't make their own food. One day they will have to. In the meantime, those who learnt to cook as children will be able to entertain and will be able to view a raw chicken as an opportunity to create an interesting meal rather than a threatening UFO. Sewing too is underrated.

Many of the things that children need to learn how to do won't win them prizes or applause, but they will be a great help and give them an ability to relate to other people. These are the voluntary activities, the ways in which children can give back to their community – helping sort out the clothes in a local charity shop, or guiding younger children to good reads in the library. Often they call for no special talents, and are delightful for the non-competitive child.

Frequently, the point is not so much what children do, more what they develop – namely, a sense that they can be active and useful, rather than sitting passively in front of a screen eating crisps and intermittently complaining of being bored if there is no shopping expedition in prospect.

'What you are good at when you are young may not be what you do when you are grown up,' says novelist Poe Brosnan. At school he was considered a genius at maths, and took part in the 'mathletic' competitions that are as popular as spelling bees in the USA. That changed when he was eighteen and he shifted his focus to writing, but what he had developed as a child was not so much an aptitude for mental arithmetic as the knowledge of how exciting it can be to try hard at something.

## What activity will suit a child?

There are several factors to take into account before opting for any activity.

**External resources.** This means several things, including what is available in the area, and what you can provide – not just as a teacher, but as a parent helping the child to develop.

**Inner resources.** Does your child have the habits, such as concentration or the ability to get over disappointments, to deal with problems and setbacks realistically and positively? Children vary more than parents realise. If you don't know whether a child can cope with an activity, a few trial sessions will soon make it obvious.

**Talent.** When my children were very young I, like most parents, thought that they were naturally gifted at almost everything, just because they could kick a ball or bash a bongo vaguely rhythmically. With older children it is easier to spot a real aptitude. A friend who noticed her son vaulting over the gate signed him up to high-jump lessons, and he is now mastering the 'Fosbury flop'.

Noël doesn't think parents should be too hung up on talent, since most children, with the right help, can reach a reasonable level at virtually anything.

**Temperament.** Children vary more than most parents, certainly parents with a first or only child, realise. Whether a child is sociable or clingy, eager to try new things or frightened by loud noises, there is a tendency to see your own child as a universal norm. In fact, of course, children are as varied as adults, and, unless you take individual characteristics into account, you may find a mismatch between an activity and the child or between the child and the teacher. A fearful child, for example, might take better to a sport such as gymnastics, which is pure technique, rather than to one that involves a ball flying at you, such as cricket.

If your child is uncomfortable in social groups, your aim may be to teach her to be more gregarious, so a solitary activity would not be desirable. But the group would have to be small, and your approach to easing the child into it would have to be gentle.

'Typical problems are caused by a clash between the child's temperament and the responses of parents, teachers and coaches,' says Noël. 'A highly sensitive or highly strung child will want to stop an activity if she has a teacher who gets annoyed easily; with a calm teacher she would learn how to come in from the edges.

'The best way to identify your child's characteristics is to observe her in relation to other children of the same age. What skills does she lack, what stage is she at, where might help be needed?'

## What matters to me?

Often parents rate as important those activities that they know and love themselves. Musical parents, for example, frequently start their children on instruments and singing at a very early age. When whole families share a love of something it can be a great bonding experience, though parents have to be wary of channelling a child into something that he doesn't enjoy just because they love it themselves.

Similarly, parents sometimes press their offspring into activities that they wish they had been acquainted with as a child. Having had relatively narrow options myself, my scattergun approach has been driven by a desire to give my children as wide a choice as possible. One drawback to this is that the parent who is as new to skating as the child won't be able to share and encourage, only observe – unless she is willing to fall flat on her back herself.

Then there are the ideas that strike parents as important because they have read the latest educational research. Languages (we are now told, though we always guessed) are best started young – as they are in many continental European countries. Before a child can read or write he is able to acquire a second language through listening. Even if he doesn't keep it up, he will have acquired a good accent and lost the self-consciousness that inhibits older children. Primary schools are beginning to recognise this; at my children's they do a little Italian, and the school office is labelled the *segreteria*, but to acquire more than a smattering of words, a parent would have to engage an au pair or find a class.

What might matter to a parent could be giving a child the confidence to stand on stage and speak. 'Character building' is the reason given by most parents (like myself) who fork out for Stagecoach's considerable fees. With secondary school children learning increasingly from computer screens at the pace of their 'individual learning plans' – and gossiping in the evenings with friends via computer chatrooms – there is a need for activities that teach children to speak up and out, to communicate clearly and feel comfortable with a moderate amount of limelight.

Keeping a child fit could be the primary aim. One mother who could see that her son was naturally greedy and might well end up overweight made an early decision that she would insist he did several sports. A parent with a particularly slothful child might also take the same line.

## What am I trying to achieve?

Parents often want to find non-academic activities for a child who is doing less well at school than his siblings. Those who have all-boy or all-girl families, or whose children attend single-sex schools might be looking for ways to get their child involved in mixed activities.

Many parents, when their child is four or five, are already thinking ahead to their later education. Often these parents want a child to go to a private school but can't afford the fees, so they are looking for a scholarship. If they don't think their child will win an academic one, they might look at art, sports or music. (In fact, if parents look around, there are scholarships of surprising kinds available, including a chess scholarship to Millfield and a riding scholarship to Bedgebury.)

Music and choral scholarships are widely available, thus presenting a reasonably large target to hit, and bringing generous discounts off the normal fees. Parents of children who have won such scholarships tell me that a child doesn't need to be musically gifted to get one, but he will have to be trained from an early age. Choristers (girls as well as boys are now accepted in some choirs) usually start aged seven. They get a wonderful musical education, though some complain in later life about the regimentation. Having a chorister also demands parental sacrifice, since most choirs insist that children board and work at weekends, and, of course, sing at Christmas.

As for instrumentalists, they have to have proven ability in at least one instrument to a fairly high level. A good Grade 2 result will get you nowhere. This means getting cracking early.

Another parental aim might be to equip a child to be a social success. I know one mother who set out to make her children the perfect weekend guests. Every holiday she would sign them up for weeks learning different skills and would brook no nonsense if they protested. Those children can now swim, ride, ski, sail, sketch and even shoot. They are so used to having their time organised for them that she says they have a tendency to ask, 'What are we doing this week?' rather than making their own fun. But she has achieved her aim: they have plenty of invitations.

Or it may even be that you want your children to earn money. Modelling with small children can be lucrative, if your child has the right temperament and characteristics – sunny, unflappable, smallish for his or her age, relaxed with strangers and attractive. There is plenty of work, especially for those who live in London, but it does mean a major commitment from the parent, who has to keep the child looking pristine and cart him or her around to the auditions.

## What's out there?

There's an old army saying that time spent on reconnaissance is never wasted. One mother who visited each of twenty possible schools for her children not once but twice was possibly slightly overdoing it, but she was essentially right. She wanted to find the perfect fit for her daughter, and she knew that places often look different on a second viewing, once you have seen the competition. There may be four different football clubs in the area, but each will have a different atmosphere, depending on the pitch, the management and the coach. Some put more emphasis on competitive matchplay, others foster basic skills; some mix boys and girls, others are single sex.

Location obviously plays a part in a parent's choices for a child, but it would be strange to encourage a child to take up go-karting if you think it is expensive and dangerous just because there is a track nearby.

What you can accommodate is another key issue. One mother thought her child could learn the piano from a keyboard – some teachers will accept them, at least with beginners. However, since the mother wasn't prepared to have the keyboard taking up space in the house, the child had to take it out of the box each time, so rarely practised.

Nor is there any point paying for Suzuki violin lessons if you don't have the time to attend the lessons yourself and make sure the practice is done. One mother e-mailed me aghast after her son's first term: 'Went to M's cello teacher the other day. All her students play for each other. An eight-year-old began with one entire Bach suite from memory. Another eight-year-old ended with two movements from the Boccherini cello concerto. In between were several prodigies aged from five to eleven. I'm still in shock. Fifteen out of the eighteen kids were Asian, and their accompanist parents seemed to be virtuosi pianists.'

She decided to give her children the chance to perform to a similarly high standard but, as she wrote, 'The music is killing me.'

## Matching the child to the activity

Cerebral children often feel useless at team games, and dislike contact sports that make them feel their personal space has been invaded. They prefer to do things on their own and aren't keen on confrontation. At school, says Lori Ferguson of the National Association for Gifted Children, such children are often bullied and laughed at for being unsporty 'boffs', and she finds that they tend to prefer tactical individual sports, such as fencing or a martial art. 'Usually you have to take the child kicking and screaming because he may see the martial art as aggressive,' she says, 'but they come to enjoy it. They may never use it, but they feel they could if challenged.'

Within sports there are subtle distinctions that make one more suitable than another for particular children. A watersports coach explained that the child who enjoys sailing is usually different in nature from the one who loves canoeing. Sailing at the simplest dinghy level is a single-handed activity, but paddling a canoe with someone else is more sociable. Although sailing might seem hard for some children, the coach assured me that he was able to build up their confidence from the beginning with simple exercises, such as swimming tests.

Of course, parents aren't just making one choice for their children. They may find several activities that provide a child with a variety of experiences. Often one activity can feed into and help progress with another. With sports, for example, a child who loves football will find that badminton, running, judo and gym also develop the twisting and turning, balance and pace needed in soccer. Swimming and golf, however, don't – but that's no reason not to do them too.

## What school gaps can be filled?

With schools selling off playing fields and the curriculum narrowing, many gaps are opening up. Parents might want to fill these to ensure that their children are getting a well-rounded start in life and acquiring the habits and basic skills that will give them a wide choice of hobbies and pleasures.

Some sports, such as tennis, require expert coaching and a court. Even if tennis is taught at school, the size of a class makes it hard for a child to get a reasonable amount of play, so tennis may best be learnt outside school.

Swimming with the whole class can be frightening for a sensitive child. The noise and splashing of all those children in the pool together can put the child off. That child might be more confident if, from an early age, long before learning at school, he had got over his fear of the water in informal private lessons.

Or it may be that a parent wants a child to share a love of rugby. Many schools don't play it, so the parent has to take the initiative.

## What can I afford?

One mother described how she applied ruthless economics to choosing holiday activities for her children. She worked out how much they cost per day against the cost of paying for childcare while she was at work. Mostly the activities won.

By any other yardstick, however, many of the activities available for children are hideously expensive. It is worth being realistic about this before the child becomes so caught up in, say, riding that it would cause deep distress to admit that the weekly outing on Trigger is proving crippling to the family budget. A recent survey of children's hobbies showed that the most expensive one for boys was moto-cross, and I can think of other good reasons, such as danger, for leaving that one well alone.

Some apparently cheap activities, such as skating, become expensive once you have got past the basic stage and require one-to-one tuition, plus skating boots and special dresses. Ballet, too can become more of a drain on the purse than it first appears because if a child is to go any distance, he or she will require not one but several lessons a week, since practising at home is discouraged. In addition, of course, there are the ballet shoes and tutus that ratchet up the cost.

Anything provided by a local authority, or a football club scouting for talent and supporters, is usually reasonably priced. Football, tennis, swimming, gymnastics and judo are all cheap in my area (a group tennis lesson costs just £2; football is £3.50). Anything provided by private enterprise – dance, drama and, of course, individual instrument lessons – is more costly.

Many parents plunge into instrument lessons without working out the true cost. There are some wonderfully cheap instruments; you can get a recorder for £10 and an OK violin for £100. Pianos come more expensive; our basic upright was £1200. Anything brass or woodwind is pricey, which I hadn't realised when I allowed a child to start oboe. Within weeks letters were coming home from the teacher about buying an instrument costing £1100. (It seems harder to hire woodwind instruments than string ones.)

If you are going to invest that much, you have to require the child to stick with it. Although you can buy and sell instruments on eBay, my experience has not been encouraging. We bought a dud and sold it again for rather less than we paid.

## Will an activity give a child confidence?

Parents often imagine that an activity will give a child not so much a skill as a confidence boost. They think that a weekly Kumon maths class will make the child feel less stupid during maths lessons, or that being able to swim will make him feel less like a loser. Confidence, we assume, comes from acquiring skills, making new acquaintances, facing challenges and learning to cope in an unfamiliar place.

It doesn't seem to be so straightforward. Feeling you have cracked something, such as tennis or chess, can certainly boost the spirits, but one of the points Noël makes repeatedly is that confidence doesn't come from success, but from self-reliance and parental approval. 'The confident child,' she says, 'feels his parents accept him for who he is, not for who they would like him to be.'

But certainly acquiring a new skill can be a boost, especially if a child is not doing well in other areas. For confidence building, it helps to start a child young, as teenagers can't bear to be seen being bad at something. Parents must be realistic about what a child can achieve, must listen reflectively to their fears and give masses of descriptive praise as the child takes each tentative step forward.

Sometimes, for the sake of a child's confidence, you have to decide that, however carefully you chose it, this is not the right activity/teacher/group/time of day/level of difficulty/ type of activity (e.g. team rather than individual sport) for your child.

## What about the child's wishes?

Parents get confused about how much of a say a child should have in choosing an extra-curricular activity. Noël is quite clear on that point: 'Children know what they want (or what they think they want), but parents know what they need. Often children have unrealistic expectations: they think they will be able to learn things far more quickly than they can. If the parent doesn't know that, the child will try something, assume she will be able to do it quickly, and then blame the guitar or the teacher when he can't.'

She gave me a list of the reasons why a child might want to do an activity, and described why most of them are fraught with potential disappointment:

- Because she can already do it well.
- To improve.
- Because it is something new.

- To please parents. (This tends to lead to high anxiety levels, even if the child is successful.)
- To be popular. (Sadly, it rarely works. Popularity is incredibly subtle; you have to aspire in just the right way.)
- Wanting to be part of a group. (This might or might not work. Noël remembers a boy who joined a swimming team, hoping to make friends. Unfortunately, only five minutes of the hour were for splashing around and, because he didn't know the others well, he couldn't muster the courage to join in the splashing.)
- To compete. (If she is trying to prove to herself that she is OK, it likely to turn into the opposite of a win–win situation. If the child doesn't win, she will feel bad. But even if the child does win, it is likely to provide only a short-lived ego boost. Victory won't cheer the child long-term: if an activity is not the cause of insecurity, it can't be the solution.)
- To feel better about themselves. (Many unconfident children feel that if only they could find something at which they shine, they will become confident. It doesn't work like that. What builds confidence is competence in everyday life rather than excellence in one thing. You can feel confident even if you are not amazing at anything, and you can feel un-confident if you have a remarkable talent but your mother constantly says you don't know your right from left.)
- Whim. (A recipe for disaster. The child needs to have a taster; don't buy the pony or the saxophone right away. If the reality is good, it supersedes the silly reason; if bad, it puts the child off. Watching someone else is a good way of having a taster: a lot of children would decide against learning the piano if they sat through half of someone else's lesson.)
- Excitement. (Often it's not the actual activity that is exciting, but dressing up or the audience. If so, find another way to provide that kind of excitement, as the kit or the performance is never going to be a major part of the activity.)
- Copying someone the child knows, or a famous person, or what parents used to do.

## Problems created by a child's preferences

Football is now the fastest-growing sport for girls, and few parents would stamp on an interest on the grounds that it unfeminine. Despite the huge success of the film, and now the musical of *Billy Elliot*, boys still encounter parental reservations when they show a real love of dance. They can be teased at school, and many dance-mad boys are home educated because of it – until they can go to one of the specialist dance schools.

Sometimes a child comes to love something that may not be good for her. Modelling, for example, encourages a preoccupation with appearance. It also means a child taking time off school, and frequently makes classmates envious, so the child is then teased. The child's liking for it doesn't necessarily mean she should be allowed to carry on.

A child may also ask to do something for which he has no aptitude. Rather than refuse, Noël suggests that a parent should make sure the child has the basic skills, and move carefully so he is successful from the beginning. Many high achievers have had to overcome enormous obstacles. Long-distance runner Paula Radcliffe is asthmatic; Alison Williamson, who won an Olympic bronze medal for archery, is so short-sighted that the target is a yellow blur; Evelyn Glennie, the percussionist, is deaf; and Wimbledon champion Maria Sharapova is not nearly as powerful as Serena Williams, yet she still beat her.

## Saying 'No' to a child

It isn't easy. A mother told me she suffered 'torments' when her daughter wanted to go to an after-school jazz class that all her friends were going to. 'Why did I say no? Because it meant shelling out more money than I felt comfortable about, and the time did not suit me. I needed to be at home then with the two younger children, giving them a bath and reading them stories. Who would take precedence? Was it all right to tell her that she couldn't, although the child – and almost every mother in the community – was vehemently opposed to my harsh decision?

'I felt my daughter was already doing enough and that she needed time to lie on her bed and escape into a childhood world of fantasies, to stare at the ceiling collecting her thoughts, that there must still be "time to see when woods we pass . . . time to turn at Beauty's glance, time to stand and stare for soon there will not be".

'I don't regret the decision, although I felt harsh at the time. I want to encourage my children to resist the urge to submit to peer pressure. We give in to that urge far too often for fear of feeling like a substandard parent if our children don't have as much, or do as much, as other children. We teach children that it is right to say "No" to something that doesn't feel right, yet we break our backs (and our bank accounts) giving in to them over things that we don't believe in.'

The mother stuck to her guns and is glad that she did so. 'Three days after the offending jazz class, my daughter had forgotten she was not part of it. And, because she didn't go, we were able to read Roald Dahl's *The Enormous Crocodile* together, and she was able to tell me about her lesson on the Incas. Because she didn't go, she is not less of a person and I am not less of a mother. She also learnt a good lesson – that it is OK to be a bit different sometimes.'

I had to find a way of saying 'No' gently when one of my children wanted to be a model. I didn't like the idea, not least because the agency booker explained that it would involve taking time off school, which I would have to pretend was due to sickness. I didn't want just to squash the child's dream, so I took her along to the agency. The booker said she would gladly put her in their catalogue, since she was the right size and shape, but asked whether she would enjoy going out after school to meet clients who might want to use her in a campaign. Luckily I knew my child well enough to know how she would react.

As I anticipated, he was extremely shy at the agency. On the way home she said she would hate having to meet all the casting agents so she no longer wanted to do it. She hasn't mentioned it again and fortunately she feels the decision was hers.

Many parents are agonised when they have to trample on a

child's dreams, as often happens when a child wants to go to a vocational school. Sometimes they may question for years whether they did the right thing. One dancer who was offered a coveted place at a specialist stage school was devastated when her parents insisted she go to a grammar school instead as they didn't want their academic daughter gambling her future on such a narrow career path. 'As a child, I felt I didn't have much of a voice,' she says several years on. 'By the time I was fourteen I had become a rebel and by fifteen I was a full-blown troublemaker. I felt I had missed the boat. I had lost confidence in my ability to perform.'

In her case there was a happy ending. After a difficult adolescence she became a television presenter. 'My foray into dance had enriched me in more ways than I could ever have understood,' she says now. 'The memory skills required to remember long dance routines stood me in good stead for remembering long pieces to camera; I had learnt the ability to perform when all around is falling apart. Even my early attempts at choreography had taught me to visualise, compartmentalise and organise, and the passion for music that I had discovered through dance imbued me with a sense of rhythm and musical awareness.'

## Finding a compromise

While Noël firmly supports parents who have come to a considered decision about what they feel is right for their child, she often finds that there is a compromise position if they reflectively listen to a child's feelings.

Sometimes a child may say she desperately wants a pony, which is often out of the question because of the cost and the effort involved. However, if you find out what the child really longs for, it may turn out that riding once a month will satisfy the craving, or that there is someone nearby willing to share a pony.

Noël once taught a teenager who horrified his parents when he announced that he wanted to drop out of school and be a ski bum. When they calmed down and discussed his longing to ski, they came to an agreement that if he stayed at school and applied for university, in his gap year he could train to be a ski instructor. With that training he was not only able to ski, but he could also support himself through university.

I too have often found that children will compromise if you discuss a plan in a calm voice, and involve them, if they are old enough to understand, in the financial aspects of a choice or ask for a contribution from their pocket money.

## Is it good to let a child appear on television?

I've always been wary about giving children fifteen minutes of fame for fear that it would become addictive. I don't mind them doing local performances, or appearing on news vox pops about Father Christmas, but I wouldn't seek out a spot for them on television. Andrew Graystone, who trains adults to appear on the media, told me I was wrong. As a child, he had appeared frequently as a singer, and he recommends it.

'It should be part of every child's education,' he says. 'Appearing on television changes their view of television from something that's passive into something that has been made by people. It shows them that people on TV are real, and they will watch it afterwards with more understanding.'

If a child has a favourite programme, he would encourage parents to write in to the producer, asking if the child can be in the audience, or even take part. If the child has a talent – say magic tricks or tap dancing – he would let them show it off. 'It's not pushy; it's making a connection,' he says.

## What is the best age to start a musical instrument?

There are two schools of thought. Teachers using the Suzuki method like to start children as young as possible, using specially adapted instruments (including a doubled-back flute), so that children acquire an understanding of music as if it were just another language. Two years old is not too soon, though, as one mother told me, 'At that age the contents of the nose can be more interesting than the activities of the group.'

The younger a child starts, the more a parent has to be involved. A child can't handle the practice alone until aged seven or eight, and parents are required to attend lessons so that they understand the method. That means flogging across town once a week, as well as daily practice supervision.

The advantages of the Suzuki method are that the children get off to a flying start, that they learn by listening to a wide repertoire, that they play together in a group and that there is little emphasis on passing exams.

Not having the time or energy for that, I was relieved to read *The Right Instrument for Your Child* by Atarah Ben-Tovim and Douglas Boyd. They recommend waiting until a child is around seven, by which time he will have developed better coordination and have got over the psychological stress of starting school. Children who try to read music sooner, they say, can develop a mental block about musical notation, as it hard for them to grasp. Children who start playing later, they say, make faster progress, and that keeps them motivated.

The book, as the title suggests, also offers a method of choosing a suitable instrument for a child based on her physique, mentality and personality. A sociable child, for example, might not like a self-contained instrument such as the guitar or piano. Hyperactive children can be a nightmare for violin teachers, but can make great percussionists. Children who are good at mental arithmetic often dislike single-note instruments, but enjoy making chords.

Some instruments, say the authors, are uncomfortable for certain builds, while brass ones are very good for the left-handed – though you need adult front teeth to play them. Having arrived at a short list, they suggest taking the child along to a shop to test the options before making the final choice.

**Note:** When choosing an instrument, it is worth remembering the 'endangered' ones, which include the bassoon, tuba, trombone, double-bass, oboe and French horn. A child who learns one of these will find it easier to get into an orchestra because there's less competition. (But also note that these endangered instruments can be more expensive to buy.)

With my own children and music I have managed an uneasy compromise. Some have asked to start instruments before the age of seven and I have let them because I am so delighted by their enthusiasm. However, I don't have much time to supervise practice, so progress is often slow. Hearteningly for late starters, the most committed musician in the family only picked up the guitar aged ten.

## Is it essential to start young?

It often helps to get going before fear or embarrassment sets in. Think of the four-year-olds who glide past adults on the ski slopes, or the children who seem to have been born in the saddle. You want to start riding before a child feels fear of the horse, and swimming before a child gets scared of drowning. Gymnasts need to start young to develop flexibility.

Technical skills have to be acquired early. No dancer has taken her first lesson at the age of seventeen. That doesn't mean that all would-be actors should go to stage schools. They suit those aiming for a career in musical theatre rather than straight acting, which is an interpretative art rather than a technical skill. Many actors only discovered their talent in their late teens, and are glad to have had a broad education first. Coordination sports (such as tennis, football, golf or squash) are best started at the age of seven or eight, though it is normal to take up rugby (which can terrify younger children) aged eleven.

But it is rarely too late for the gifted and determined. Recently a seventeen-year-old won a scholarship to Harrow on the strength of his cricketing. He had arrived in the UK only five years previously, speaking no English and having never played the game. One of the British boxers at the Athens Olympics only picked up the gloves aged fourteen, although nine is a more normal age to start. Catherine Bishop, a gold medallist rower at Athens, hadn't touched an oar before she went to Cambridge to read music and modern languages. Long hours spent practising the cello, she said, had taught her how to concentrate.

---

**WHAT'S POSITIVE?**
- Giving a child opportunities to taste activities one at a time, without throwing them at him.
- Not assuming that children have the same tastes and temperament as yourself.
- Feeling responsible to a child, not for him.
- Setting short-term goals that are difficult enough to give a sense of achievement, but within the child's grasp.
- Allowing a child to decide after an agreed trial period whether she wants to carry on.
- Setting a date for a review. Maybe a child has to stick to something for a year before deciding whether to continue.

---

**WHAT'S PUSHY?**
- Signing up children for too many things, e.g. ballet on Monday, swimming on Tuesday, Kumon maths on Wednesday . . . Children who grow up expecting the world to be constantly stimulating will find it disappointing.
- Insisting a child concentrate on one activity to the exclusion of all others.
- Being unrealistic about what a child can achieve.

# 4

## MOTIVATION

Why do children want to try something?
What do I do if a child doesn't want to start something?
How do I foster enthusiasm in a child?
What do I do if a child starts saying after a while that he
doesn't want to keep going?
When should I let a child stop?

Usually it is not a problem to get a child to try something new if
he has stumbled upon the activity himself. Getting a child to try
something that a parent thinks is a good idea can be more
difficult – as can sustaining a child's enthusiasm when the novelty
of a new activity palls.

A recent report said that parents in the UK spend £12 billion on
their children's hobbies. That's a great deal of money, particularly in
view of the fact that, as researchers found, more than half of those
new activities are abandoned after just five weeks.

My own children certainly tend to rush into new activities –
dozens of them. Being eager for them to find their talents, I
almost always allow them to try something that takes their fancy
or mine – unless it is too expensive (say, horse riding) or involves
my having to spend the whole of Saturday in the car each week to
get them to an activity (say, horse riding again). Fortunately,
none of my children has got the pony bug – yet.

Sometimes they get fed up very soon. Kumon maths –
excellent though it is if a child is struggling with numeracy or is
intensely interested – was one of those that I let slip when I saw

the commitment to daily practice that it demanded from both parent and child. A French club, too, went by the wayside when I found that the children weren't learning a tremendous amount. At least, having done it for a few terms, the children could say a few sentences without dying of embarrassment.

But I am not always happy for them to give things up. It doesn't matter to me one jot if they learn to skate (well, maybe one jot), but it does matter if they learn to solve a problem without giving up. We all want children to develop staying power. That means making a decision to do something and then having the determination to get through the inevitable bad bits: to keep going when a lesson clashes with a party or the weather turns bad or the child falls out with one of the others in the group.

If children are to get anywhere with tennis, football or piano lessons, they will have to develop self-motivation. Parents can motivate to the extent of getting the child going, setting rules and being firm about attendance. But at some point the child has to decide for herself that this is what she wants to do. It's the child's motivation that matters, not the parents', if she is going to make the most of an opportunity.

Talent alone is never enough. A natural aptitude for something, whether sport, maths or creative writing, will mean that the early stages come easily, but the later stages of honing a talent require commitment. A talent is just a starting point, a reassurance that if you put in the work you might get somewhere. No doubt David Beckham showed tremendous promise as a five-year-old, but the real secret of his success, Luke Scott points out, is that he has always put in an extra hour's training after other team members have headed for the showers or the bar.

The Football Association's definition of motivation is 'the intensity and direction of a player's behaviour'. With intensity and direction, a child can go further than anyone ever thought possible. You don't have to be a prodigy to win a music or art scholarship (as many parents will testify), but you do have to have developed the habit of working hard at that subject so you can be a useful member of the orchestra or a keen sketcher.

When a child feels successful at something or has his eye on an eventual goal, motivation can be almost effortless. Billie Piper left home when she was twelve and lodged with a great aunt while attending the Sylvia Young Theatre School. It was, she has said, 'hard work and lonely at times, but it was what you wanted so you didn't think: "God, I'm so tired, I've had only six hours' sleep." You thought: "More singing. More dancing. More cabaret." I was just very ambitious.'

Motivation is a habit that is well worth acquiring. extra-curricular activities teach it better than schoolwork. At school a child has to decide to learn something, but the child is required to attend and the teachers are paid to put into action systems of rewards and consequences. Outside school it is up to the parent to train a child to understand that what you put into something is what you get out, that there are pain barriers to be crossed and that time is to be invested wisely, not frittered away.

The habit of motivation and the willingness to delay gratification that is developed by sport and artistic activities can be transferred to adult life. A tennis player who skipped university only to find she didn't become a grand slam winner then became a history student. She got a first-class degree, which she puts down to knowing how to focus and use her time. She went on to a successful career as a banker because she understood about winning and losing, and about not letting either go to your head.

## What motivates a child?

There are two reasons why a child starts a new activity: either he wants to do it or the parent thinks the activity is going to benefit him.

In the first instance the child is already motivated. With a young child it will be the activity itself that appeals. Usually it just seems like fun: all a girl's friends go to ballet, or football looks like a great excuse to roll in the mud.

Fun came first in a recent Football Association survey of such factors. Other top reasons were: 'be with mates', 'be like

Beckham', 'because my parents want me to', 'to get away from my brother' and football is 'exciting'. Winning featured at number thirty-six – which might be useful for the competitive parent to remember.

A parent who wants to motivate a child to embark on something that she thinks worthwhile has to harness the fun factor. One mother who was determined that all her children would be readers, largely so she could read again herself after 'the great hole of babyhood', encouraged them to read anything they wanted, rather than the books she considered improving. If the *Beano* was what they liked, it was fine by her. They are now in the habit of settling down to read, and she can do so too.

But sometimes it is not enough to get children into a habit for them to become self-motivating. Even if the initial impulse was one of pleasure and excitement, even if they made fast progress to begin with, as they go further, the going gets tougher, the progress slower. A child becomes more aware of his limitations than of how far he has come, and motivation drops off.

There will be times when he makes a hideous fuss because he would rather be doing something else. Perhaps he's tired. Maybe the last lesson didn't go well, or he's annoyed that someone in the group didn't pick him as a partner. The teacher may have been 'mean' to the child for chattering.

Only older children can see the point of what are called 'extrinsic' factors – that tutoring might be the way to keep up or to get into a really good secondary school, or that coaching could be the key to becoming the next Tim Henman or Tiger Woods. It might also be that getting really good at chess would be a way of beating your mother or your snooty elder brother. Or just a way of getting out of the house more, a means of earning money or of becoming famous.

## Why won't some children try new activities?

You know the ones: whatever you suggest to them, they say, 'That sounds boring.' The parent then becomes cross and may say something about the child being spoilt or lazy, which only serves to label the child in her own mind as a hopeless case. 'Unmotivated children resist learning and cooperating,' says Noël. 'This resistance is often automatic, habitual, unconscious and unreasonable.

'"I can't, I won't, I don't care," such children tell their parents. Usually, when a child can't seem to get interested in anything, it is because she lacks confidence, foresees failure or believes that there is only a point in trying something if you are going to be brilliant. Even if the child goes along to the lesson, she can resist learning anything.'

What should parents do then? 'Be more positive with the child,' she suggests. 'Build up confidence through descriptive praise of all the things a child is doing well. Also descriptively praise any small signs of those qualities you want the child to acquire, such as a willingness to try new things. Make it plain that the point of the activity in your eyes is not to be brilliant but to try. Very few are truly gifted, but the rest of us enjoy being able to do something at a level of ordinary competence.'

Descriptive praise alone will not necessarily get the child to take part in a lesson. For that the parent may have to tread slowly but firmly. Rather than shoving the child through the door and bolting, the parent might ask to watch a class with the child first of all, maybe even several weeks running, without the child taking part. After a while, the child might be willing to try sitting with the group and, eventually, will begin to join in.

'When my son went to his first karate lesson,' Noël remembers, 'the class was already going, so he felt intimidated. When the sensei [instructor] called him up, my son walked on the corner of the mat and the sensei yelled at him – it seemed to be a part of the tradition, a test of mettle.

'My son was very upset, and he was sure the teacher didn't want him in the class. I thought that the conclusion he had drawn would cripple him, so I said he must go back. I didn't say the teacher was right or wrong. If I had said the teacher was right, my son would have felt he was in the wrong, and if I had said the teacher was wrong, my son would have lost all respect for the teacher.

'So I insisted he go back, and although he was uncomfortable at first, he was very careful not to do anything wrong, and soon he came to love it.'

Sometimes, too, lack of motivation or concentration is a mask for anxiety not necessarily related to the particular activity. It can stem from the feeling that if you do something, you have to be good at it. Noël's daughter was nine when Noël suggested tennis lessons. The girl said, 'I don't want to do that.' 'Why on earth not?' Noël asked. She said, 'Because I don't know how to play tennis.' 'She didn't get it that the purpose of lessons is to learn; she thought you had to be good to start with.'

Another mother whose child was promoted to a higher ballet class because she was good found her once eager daughter suddenly anti-ballet. Again it was fear of failure. Getting the child to the first lesson in the higher class was a nightmare, but she told her daughter that she had to at least try it. She virtually pushed her through the door and spent the whole lesson outside wondering if she was a monster parent, but at the end of it the child came out happy. Her worst fears had not been fulfilled.

## Why do some children seem not to concentrate?

One of the interesting points that Noël made is that motivation and concentration are inextricably linked. 'Most people think motivation (an emotion) and concentration (a physiological skill) don't go together, but, in fact, each follows the other,' she says. 'When you are motivated, you concentrate and try to do your best; when you concentrate, you get more motivated as you see something, learn something, enjoy something. Motivation and concentration appear to be different, but are in fact almost identical: motivation is what you feel, concentrate is what you do.'

I should, perhaps, have realised this, seeing how one of my sons can concentrate for hours on guitar practice, yet at school he often has to be helped with his 'concentration problems'. No doubt there is an element of neurological difficulty when it comes to organising himself and learning through reading, but lack of motivation is probably a large part of his problem.

## Ways to encourage children to try new things

'How you increase motivation and concentration,' says Noël, 'depends on the activity, the age of the child, the purpose behind the activity and the child's temperament type. There are certain things parents can do to make all children feel braver about trying new things.

**Practise more positive communication.** Parents can often, without noticing it, say things that children experience as belittling, confusing, critical, demoralising, demotivating, discouraging, embarrassing, frightening, frustrating, infuriating, overwhelming or provocative.

When I listen to myself I am often shocked by the sarcasm and impatience that I think pass for a positive response. I say critical things such as, 'Go on, you've nothing better to do.' Or neutral things such as 'Why don't you just try?' but in a weary voice. When I concentrate on being genuinely encouraging, I notice a difference in the results.

**Descriptively praise all the tiny steps in the right direction.** Make sure to notice when a child has gone to netball practice, even though it is cold and wet and she would rather watch television. If the child makes only a partial success of something – he goes to the karate lesson but doesn't take part – praise the part you approve of and make no remark on the rest. So, 'It was good that you tried that difficult shot, even though it didn't come off' or 'Even though you were quite scared, you still gave it a try.'

**Watch your non-verbal communication.** Parents often create the wrong impression by their body language. They look cross, fold their arms and make a child feel under pressure. 'A lot of motivating can be done non-verbally,' says Noël. 'When a child is upset the parents also usually get upset and stop smiling. But when you smile it releases endorphins in both the person who is smiling and in the child who is being smiled at.'

**Don't argue or reason.** If you have decided that the child must do something, then arguing and reasoning will only weaken your case. The child is being unreasonable, so reasoning is a waste of time. Some children don't want to go to school; arguing with them does not convince them. What makes a difference is a parent who requires the child to do as expected.

**Create the right environment.** If you want a child to take exercise, take some yourself and enjoy it, otherwise exercise can feel like a pressure rather than a pleasure. Why should a child think reading is fun if you never do it, or see the point of learning the violin if classical music is never played in the home?

**Provide incentives.** These are not bribes, which are arbitrary, but rewards that a child knows he can earn; they should be given for effort as well as success. There are four types of rewards:

- Things
- Social actions (e.g. hugs, praise, smiles)
- Activities
- Tokens (e.g. a gold star, or money that goes towards something else, perhaps an outing to the pizzeria at the end of the month)

**Have realistic expectations.** Do not focus just on what can be achieved long term, but what the child can achieve in a few weeks, months or even hours.

**Spend time with the child.** A father who spends time with a child only when he is playing football will find that child less keen to please him by taking part than if they spend time together doing other things as well. 'Consistency of quality time,' says Noël, 'improves motivation and concentration.'

## What if a child is still resistant?

Parents of intense, sensitive, impulsive children, Noël finds, often give in when the child is upset. In fact, the child would feel safer and happier if the parent were to stand firm and hold steady.

'Motivation is about wanting to do something, and one of the actions that achieves motivation is requiring the child to do it,' says Noël. 'It is counter-intuitive, but it is true.'

When a parent proposes a new activity, she says, a resistant child usually goes through four stages:

- Refusal or resistance
- Complaining
- Forgetting to complain
- Enjoyment

A parent who gives up too easily would write a child out of an activity for life – an activity that a child might quite soon come to enjoy.

## What do you do when a child's enthusiasm wanes?

Every child will experience a drop in motivation at some point, however enjoyable an activity. There's nothing anyone can stay consistently thrilled about, and motivation is fragile. All sorts of things can dishearten a child, particularly if something unexpected goes wrong. It could be that the teacher tells him off, or that he's embarrassed at not doing as well as he should have done, or that the other children in the group may have made him feel left out. 'How parents handle that,' Noël says, 'will determine how and if the child continues.'

Sometimes parents say, 'It's up to you', and let the child give up. Those children learn nothing about perseverance and may become dilettantes.

Or parents may say, 'Yes, you will carry on. Think of all the money we have spent.' Those parents have made a battle out of what was just a feeling.

Another parent might plead, as if he or she didn't have the right to require the child to do something. It will be easier for the child if you decide you have the right to require her to continue.

Noël knows many parents who take a child out of an activity

at the first hint of discontent, or maybe after a few weeks. 'Mostly,' she says, 'the child then whinges about the next unfamiliar thing. When we aren't sure about something, we look for reasons or a quick fix – then the child comes up with another reason.' The child's negativity gets your attention, and it gets the child out of what was a temporary problem. So just as you would not take a child out of school, don't take him out of extra-curricular activities.

'The children who are happy to do extra-curricular activities are those who are not given a choice, whose parents aren't worrying. How you feel is going to determine how you react.

At the bottom of many parents' unwillingness to insist on what they believe to be right lies, she believes, an indulgent attitude based on a misconception. 'Many parents say they just want their children to be happy,' says Noël. 'That's laudable until it emerges that the parents want the children to be happy *all* the time.'

So when a child says something is no longer fun, the parents don't analyse what the child really means – 'not fun', like 'boring', can mean anything from too difficult to too easy. It can denote a critical coach or simply a desire to watch a television programme. (The only way to discover is to carefully unpick the meaning using reflective listening.)

'If extra-curricular activities are presented as always being fun,' Noël finds, 'children don't see why they should keep going if they aren't having fun. Then the parents get confused: they don't know whether to insist, or give the child a choice. When the child becomes resistant, it can become a battle. Then the parents start bargaining and that undermines the child's respect for the parents' authority.'

To teach children that they can be happy even when they are not getting what they want she makes a point of not letting them have something they desire. 'With a child who badly wanted to use a particular pencil,' she says, 'I gave him another one and made him carry on, and asked him at the end if it made much difference. He admitted that it didn't. That is good practice for the times when things aren't going the way you wish.'

So if you don't give in, what do you do to sort out a child who is complaining vociferously about something you have decided he has to do? Both descriptive praise and reflective listening feature on Noël's prescription for helping children through the inevitable sags in enthusiasm. 'Through reflective listening the child can be helped to get to the bottom of a feeling and eventually move through it. With reflective listening you may or may not discover anything useful,' she explains, 'but it will help the child to feel heard. That makes it easier to move on, even if you never find out what the particular problem was. The child may not even know.'

The point about reflective listening, she explains, is that it is not a way of quickly fixing a problem, but a way to help a child explore uncomfortable feelings. When Noël advised the parents of a child who was sulking and making apparently deliberate mistakes in her chess class, she told them to curb their annoyance, insist the child kept going and do lots of reflective listening. 'It may seem odd not to try to solve a problem when the solution seems easy – you just take the child out of the class – but the problem won't stay solved. The child may well bring moody responses to the next activity. The beauty of reflective listening is that it helps kids to move beyond their discomfort.'

## Some examples of motivation problems solved

One set of parents that Noël advised had a daughter who was very well suited to gymnastics: she had long, lean muscles, no body fat and was very flexible. Although she was only five, she was soon put up into a class of six-year-olds. 'The child felt great about it and so did the parents,' says Noël. 'Then she was put in a seven-year-olds' class and the parents wondered where it was going to end. The club she attended loved their pupils to win as it was a huge feather in their cap, though they were not desperate to win at the expense of its members' happiness.

'Then, quite suddenly, the girl went through a slump and didn't want to do gymnastics. The parents didn't know if she no longer enjoyed the activity, or if the pressure of competition was too great, or if she didn't like being with older children, or if she disliked being away from home so much.'

Noël's advice to the parents was to carry on with the classes and to do lots of reflective listening. The unsettled period lasted for a few months. After that, there was no problem, and it was as if there had never been one.

'But what had been the problem?' I asked. 'They never found out,' she replied. 'The parents didn't learn much from the reflective listening, the child herself didn't seem to know why she made such a fuss for four or five months. But that's how it often is in a child's life. She went on to win rosettes, do well and enjoy herself tremendously.'

Around the time Noël told me that story, my younger son had started tennis lessons. He showed a flair for it, but soon started to say that he didn't want to go any more. All week he would keep declaring that on Sunday he wouldn't be going, which made me angry.

What was it all about, I asked myself. Was it over-confidence, having been told by me that he was 'brilliant' when all I meant (being an over-excitable, proud mother) was that he was good for his age? Was it being put up a class too young and being scared of the older players? Was it the loneliness of the game compared to the team spirit of football? Was it fear of failure? Was the coach too critical? I worried that I should have let him stay with his own age group until some of the other children were also ready to move up.

After a few weeks of having him holding on to the furniture rather than go, I was tempted to abandon the fight. Noël felt that was feeble. 'Have you done the reflective listening?' she asked. 'It doesn't sound like it. Let him have his feelings without trying to argue him out of what he's feeling. Don't try to solve the problem quickly; if you try to do that, the child will still want to complain.

'It is tempting to remind the child, "You say you don't want to go to tennis, but once you are there, you always have a lovely time". It's far better to take the time to prepare for success by discussing it throughout the week, not just ten minutes before the lesson. The first time you mention to him that on Sunday he will be doing tennis you can expect a tantrum, or at least a whinge. But by the time Sunday comes around, the child will have heard this many times and got used to the idea that he is going, and he will have talked himself out.'

The tantrums drove me mad, and I suspected that he was using the tennis as a way to test his ability to manipulate me. However, after extensive reflective listening at calm moments, I found that what he disliked about the lessons was that because he attended them, I no longer felt it necessary to play tennis with him myself. Once I got back on the court with him in between lessons, he was more sanguine about the coaching.

Another story Noël tells is about a spoilt nine-year-old who was complaining about a music teacher and wouldn't practise. 'My advice to the mother was to carry on with the teacher,' she says. 'She didn't listen. Six months later, when I bumped into her, she told me triumphantly that they had switched teachers and he was now practising.

'From that I learnt to be more circumspect when I give advice. Now I would tell a parent that one possibility is to leave the boy with his teacher, reflectively listen and have faith, but another possibility is to change teachers – which might or might not work.'

## Should a parent let a child have days off?

Any regular activity is going to clash with the occasional birthday party or other enticing alternative. I can't bear to think how many hours I have spent listening to children trying to wheedle their way out of commitments. Eventually I developed an inviolable rule that each child is allowed one exception per term, maximum – and definitely no more.

Not only do I want to avoid the battles, I don't want the child to have days off because that is the quickest route to dropping out. If a child misses a lesson, she feels she looks a fool when the other are children performing a new step, so she feels excluded. Also, because the child is making a mess of the step, the teacher feels irritated and the child feels gauche.

So many parents are casual about children's attendance at extra-curricular activities – maybe they feel that because they are paying they can decide when a child attends – that those who organise them are becoming much tougher. They now take registers, give attendance stickers and awards, and send letters asking for an explanation if an absence hasn't been accounted for.

I was grateful to one of my daughters' youth theatre organisers who summoned all parents and children taking part for a talk before they signed up. 'We do not understand the word "party",' said the woman in charge, 'so don't even mention it to us. Illness and family weddings we will accommodate, but parties you will have to miss if you decide to do this on Saturday afternoons.'

Thanks to such straight talking, whenever invitations clash with youth theatre I can remind the child of the rule – actually she doesn't need reminding; she just wants to grumble and check that the rule still applies – and the subject is closed.

Usually, I find, you can squeeze in the last bit of the party after the activity or take the child along for half an hour before the party starts to help set up, which the other parents are often grateful for as it calms down the party-giver.

## Should I let a bored child give up?

'Why has he gone off the activity?' Noël asks. 'Often because practising seems like a horrible, lonely punishment. So be there with him for the practice, and let him do it in the kitchen rather than in his bedroom. If you can't be there, ask someone else to supervise the practice. Even if the au pair is not very enthusiastic, her presence is better than practising in isolation.

'The child may have gone off the lessons because he has been given the idea that he is meant to enjoy himself all the time. If he isn't having fun, he thinks he is entitled to give up. He probably has a parent who thinks that extra-curricular activities are meant to be enjoyable, and so therefore doesn't enforce practice. That child may develop a pattern of stopping and starting activities, getting hooked on instant gratification.'

In that case, she advises being firm. 'Assuming that the child was given a taster of the activity before committing himself, he should agree to give himself a year to try it. The parent should make it clear that in that year he must give himself a chance by practising regularly or else it was not a fair trial.

'To make it easier for him to muster enthusiasm, ensure the practice is properly organised and supervised, and build rewards and consequences into the routine.'

## Why do children drop out?

There are predictable ages when children give things up. They often start a lot of activities when they are tiny, and drop them when they are seven and start to bring homework back from school. Another drop-off point comes at eleven, when most children move to secondary school. 'I wish they wouldn't give up,' says my local Stagecoach organiser. 'What else are they going to spend the three hours doing? I doubt if it will be anything constructive: they'll probably just veg out or text their friends.'

One excuse children often give is that they can't see the point of something. 'In itself that's not enough,' says Noël. 'A lot of what they learn at school children can't see the point of, but we don't let them drop out of those lessons.'

Puberty is another flashpoint. Many talented girl skaters give up aged thirteen, when they no longer want to fall over and get unsightly bruises; dancers too give up at that age because they become self-conscious about their bodies or have not yet learnt to control their newly-grown limbs. Teenage boys often give up anything that appears to them uncool. They even drop out of football aged fifteen or sixteen, as they want to stay in bed on Saturday morning, or want to go out with girls. They may need some new incentive, such as working for a coaching badge, to keep them going.

'At around 16–19 I see a lot drop out,' says a top tennis coach. 'Those who have aimed high realise at that stage that they will never be pros, and they can't take the idea of just playing for fun, even though 95 per cent of club players would love to be as good as they are. Often it is ten years or more before they return to the game.'

And those who only wanted to play for fun find by their teens that the atmosphere can get too serious. The mother of a teenager who had been county standard in tennis as well as a top chess player explained why she had let him give up both activities: 'To stay in the tennis squad, he was having to play on Saturdays and have private coaching sessions. He was never going to be a future Henman. He loved being on the team, but the pressure was constant. Every day the coach asked, "Are you coming to practice tomorrow?" With chess club, too, he had to do it very seriously or not at all. So he now plays rugby at school and chess at home.'

That mother sounded uncertain about whether she had done the right thing when she added that, 'For a sporty boy he is now a bit hunched up, but in the end, if it stops being fun, you have to back off.' I suspect she wishes she had been a little firmer.

## Are there good reasons for dropping out?

Lots. It may be that an activity is just too much of a financial drain. Parents can only do so much to help a child. If something costs too much, the child has to accept it. Often, however, a horse-mad child can muck out the stables, or a sporty one can find a charitable trust to help pay for his equipment and expenses.

Sometimes an activity may also take up too much time. If it is getting in the way of school work, it may have to go by the board for a while.

And, of course, the child may not just be complaining about a temporary lack of enthusiasm – the issue of 'fun', which is soluble – but may be genuinely unhappy. Usually there is a reason outside of the activity for why something stops being enjoyable, as the game itself hasn't changed. More often than not, the problem can be traced back to the parents being insensitive or too critical.

One tennis coach told me how he wished some parents were more sensitive to their child's feelings. 'When parents won't let an unhappy child drop out at a certain level, it is usually because the parent himself has become emotionally involved,' he said. 'The child then finds himself on a treadmill.' Those children may end up rejecting the activity for the rest of their lives.

Here are some reasons why children want to drop out.

**Critical parents.** The Football Association's research shows that the main reason why kids drop out is not that the game stopped being fun, but that 'Dad shouted at me when we didn't win'. Criticism removes the fun. Encouraging and supporting are what children need. Parents need to remember that effort is more important than achievement.

**Critical coaches.** Some coaches find it as hard as some parents to distinguish between encouragement and criticism. A young athlete, who trains three times a week a long distance from home and often in the freezing cold, says that the only thing she can't bear is the attitude of the coach. 'Sometimes he is too aggressive and says things like, "Didn't I tell you that you can't do that?" Some kids and parents think that the more aggressive the coach, the more you learn, but I don't agree.'

Some coaches are critical because they don't understand what a child can or can't do at a particular age. The FA says that 7–12-year-olds, for example, can dribble and shoot, but not head, long-pass or tackle.

From twelve, the atmosphere during training at many clubs can be oppressive for the child who has an interest, but not a passion. One father was 'quite taken aback' by the football training his daughter is receiving at their local club. 'There are people wandering around with clipboards observing all the time,' he said. 'The coaches can be quite critical of any mistakes.'

If parents put pressure on the child to continue with a critical, demoralising coach, the activity becomes a source of contention between parent and child.

**Over-competitive children.** One girl who got far on the tennis circuit described why she gave it up. She could cope with the lonely times in hotels and the strain of the matches, but she couldn't bear the aggression of some of the other players. 'You see people with blood in their eyes, hissing, "I hope you die," under their breath when you change ends.'

You can't change other people's children, but you can teach your own child to behave decently – and it might even catch on.

## How can parents stop being critical?

Noël tells a story about a father and son whose relationship had gone wrong because the father had been – quite unconsciously – too pushy in the sense of being critical. 'I worked with a boy whose father was really into stamp collecting,' she says. 'The boy so wanted to bond with his dad that he had become very keen on it too, and loved all the accoutrements.

'But the father was very critical of the way his son handled the stamps and of his limited knowledge of the subject. When he went to auctions with his father he was criticised for not noticing the finer points. So the son grew to hate everything to do with stamp collecting, and the father became very upset. For the boy it had become an extra-curricular duty, not a pleasure.

'The parents came to us because the boy wouldn't revise for exams. When it came out that he had once loved stamp collecting but no longer did – and that the parents didn't know why – I talked to the boy and found out how he felt.

'At first the father didn't understand why the boy was turned off by the criticism. I asked the father not to suggest to his son that they did anything to do with stamps because the more the father suggested it, the more the boy used it as a weapon against him. Instead I encouraged the father just to pursue his own hobby, and whenever his son said anything about it, the father was to be positive. He was to say things like, "Oh, I remember how carefully you used to use the tweezers . . ." There was lots of descriptive praise, but no reflective listening, as the father wasn't prepared to do that.

'As the father–son relationship warmed up again, the father saw how he had upset the child and made him feel a failure. Over time they were able to reconnect in their love of stamps, and went on to assemble some amazing sets together. It became a real bond. The child also began revising again and did better in his exams.'

## What keeps a child motivated?

Andrew Murray, the teenage golfer who wowed the world by winning the US Open Juniors in 2004, finds it easy to analyse his commitment to the game: 'It is much easier to be motivated if you are winning,' he says.

Whatever the activity, and whatever the level, the child will need to feel some sense of success (which is not the same as winning) to keep going. One of my daughters was about to give up the oboe, a notoriously hard instrument, because she felt she was useless. Then she was put in an all-abilities orchestra at school. Now I almost wish she *had* given up, as I am being badgered to buy her an extremely expensive instrument.

It is important for the child to aim high, but to be realistic. A child who aims to play for England rather than get into the third eleven is doomed to give up. Certainly, he won't get anywhere near the first eleven unless he aims at one achievable step after another. Often it is easier for children to be dogged about developing a talent if they are not doing so well in other areas – academically, perhaps. The child who has many talents often finds it harder to decide which one to put his energy into.

Boredom is also useful for motivating children to keep up an interest. The French actress Emmanuelle Béart (*Manon des Sources*) was brought up in the depths of the country with no TV, theatre or cinema, so she learnt to be an actress by watching others very carefully – their voices, gestures, the way they walked. Unfortunately, most children have so many distractions that it is hard for them to be motivated: a child who watches a lot of TV or plays computer games for hours may feel too lethargic to do anything more constructive.

---

**HOW TO BOOST SAGGING INTEREST**
- Provide a short-term goal – a concert, a match, a tournament. These do not have to be high-powered. My children were as excited at putting together a little concert for an old people's home as they would have been if they were playing at the Wigmore Hall.
- Exams and diplomas not only provide a focus, they also make sure that the essential building blocks of know-ledge have not been missed out in the rush to succeed.
- Let a child change and develop. A shift from one instrument to another can restore a child's musical interest, and a parent needn't feel that years of lessons have been wasted. The child will pick up the second instrument quickly. Or let a classical pianist shift to jazz piano. It's not the end of the world, and there are more jobs playing in bars, where he can earn some money. It's much better to play something that you are enjoying or that gives you peer status.
- It may be time to change the teacher. No one wants or, indeed, needs the same teacher throughout.
- Give a psychological boost. A new music stand, goggles or racket can do the trick.

---

## And a motivational exercise . . .

Luke Scott's analysis of motivation is that it is all about learning to make your commitment more important than the negative feelings that are bound to intrude. He has a way of explaining this to young people that he learnt when working with troubled teenagers at Youth at Risk. There he worked through an exercise with them that helped them to understand what was involved in motivation. The exercise is known as 'Coach/Player/Critic'.

The child is the Player, who is committed to a particular goal – say, being the fastest sprinter in the world. 'The kid needs to sign up for that,' says Luke, 'to decide that's what he wants more than anything. Success in anything depends on motivation and that means being committed. It can be quite tricky: sometimes the parents think the child is committed to a goal, and want him to be committed, but he isn't. A four-year-old is only committed to having fun. Even most fourteen-year-olds don't automatically have the maturity to commit to learning something that may be difficult at times. This exercise helps children to develop the ability to commit.

'We discuss the role of the Coach, which is to teach the Player, but the Coach can only do that with the Player's permission. The Coach keeps reminding the Player of his commitment, and tries to remove anything that gets in the way of the commitment. The Player doesn't have to like or agree with the Coach, but he does have to give permission to be coached. The Coach, who is watching the Player, can see things that the Player can't see. So if the Coach says, "You're going to need to eat this kind of food," the Player will do as he says. Sprinters, for example, aren't going to like doing a two-mile run before breakfast, but they must do it, not to please the Coach, but because they are committed to a goal.

'The third element is the Critic. This is who the Player becomes when he is thinking about himself. The Critic is the little negative voice he hears in his own head which says, "Let's not bother to practise today", "This is too hard", "It's cold" or "I know my coach said no chips but . . ." This negative voice undermines us and stops us achieving.

'The point of training,' Luke continues, 'is to teach us to take less and less notice of that negative voice. Eventually you think, "I'm a professional, I've got a job to do." Training is about learning to go with the commitment rather than with the feelings.'

Going with the feelings, in his view, is a disease of modern life. 'That's why marriages are in such trouble: we forget that we made a commitment to get through difficult times. In the context of work and achievement, it's part of the quick success culture. When you talk to really successful people, you find they have slogged for years learning their craft. Those who have built up hotel chains started in the kitchens doing the dishes, just as many pop stars trained and danced and sang for years before their lucky break.'

## Can a child be too motivated?

Children who believe they have discovered their passion in life at an early age – as I know from one of mine – can often want to concentrate on that to the exclusion of all the other things that a parent would like the child to do or learn. It can be worrying to feel that a child is narrowing his options and possibly relying on a talent that might not take him as far as he hopes. Drive without sufficient talent is just as heartbreaking as talent squandered.

Noël would use the child's motivation as a lever to make sure that he does other things too, for as long as possible. She once had a severely dyslexic pupil who had a lead role in a West End musical. She couldn't write or spell, but she loved to act. 'When I saw her in drama class I could see she had a natural gift for it,' she says. 'The girl went to a stage school, where she was having difficulty coping with the academic work. Her parents were considering sending her to a different stage school, one with lower academic standards. As long as they were talking about that as a possibility, the girl had the option of not trying her best.

'Then they decided that if she left this stage school, she couldn't go to another. She knew then that to stay at the school she had to improve her writing and spelling. It meant that she had to apply herself to something extremely difficult for her, but she was willing to do it once she saw that her parents were serious when they said they wouldn't find another stage school for her.'

This story reinforces Noël's belief that, 'Kids expect parents to be in charge, to make decisions. Even when parents have lost a child's respect, they can regain it without losing a smidgen of love by making a decision and sticking to it.'

## What should a parent do when a child is desperate to do an activity?

Children often say they are desperate to do something. Sometimes this is just because 'all' their friends are doing it; but it can also be a deep-seated and personal desire. The only way to find out is over time.

A mother of a boy at a ballet boarding school told me how reluctant she had been for her son to dance full time. As a small child, he had seemed to love music, so she sent him to ballet, but he gave up at the age of five because there were so few other boys. Then, at the age of eight, he saw Wayne Sleep give a workshop at the Royal Academy of Dance, and he wanted to start again.

'I delayed as I felt it was a big deal for a boy, wearing tights and being the only boy in the class,' she says, 'but he was so determined that I couldn't stand in his way. He's now happy among other boys who share his interest. I've seen my role throughout as to give him confidence without telling him what to do. Is that being a pushy parent?'

---

**PUSHY PARENTS DESTROY MOTIVATION BY . . .**
- Starting children on too many activities at once. It is hard to feel motivated about all of them.
- Bombarding the child with advice and lessons as soon as he shows an interest in an activity. The child soon feels overwhelmed and wishes he hadn't even mentioned that it might be nice to try sailing.

---

- Putting too much drive behind getting a child to succeed. The drive must come from within the child. Shirley Brashier, a former winner of the French Open tennis tournament, says: 'You have to be able to take the pressure, make the decisions, play when you don't feel like it.'
- Doing too much for your child. Many children lack self-discipline because the parents have made life too easy for them.
- Thinking that putting pressure on children will help them do well. Many golf courses ban parents from pulling trolleys in junior competitions because they cause too many upsets.
- Forgetting that a child has to like doing something to put his all into it.
- Focusing on results rather than effort.
- Giving children what they ask for too soon; they should have to invest their time and determination in becoming better in order to earn the new equipment.

# 5

## WINNING AND LOSING

How do I train a child to become a good winner or loser?
How to stop a child being a perfectionist?
Are exams a good idea?

Many schools nowadays foster a culture of minimal competition. Exam results are no longer posted up on notice boards; they are kept private and anonymised. Sports days consist of fun games designed to ensure that no one gets too upset. Children are protected from losing as if it would cause irreparable psychological damage. Some call it institutionalised mollycoddling. Others say it is part of the prevailing anti-boy ethos.

No doubt those children who always come last, academically or at sports, are the happier for not having their noses rubbed in their shortcomings. But one reason why many parents are keen for their children to take part in extra-curricular activities is that it gives them a chance to get used to winning.

The parent who wants a child to experience competition may be the one whose starring moments were as a competitive child, but such parents are right in many ways. There is nothing so exciting as success. Goals motivate children to try their best, whereas honing skills for their own sake can get tedious.

Every parent wants his or her child to taste success, but fewer want them also to taste the more bitter flavour of defeat. Child psychologist Michelle Elliot sees many parents going to great lengths to prevent their children from experiencing setbacks. She thinks this is a mistake: 'In the process, they create an illusion that children can achieve anything. Occasional failures can come as a shock later in life, when the youngsters are on their own and don't have parents constantly providing the stimulus and support.'

Success, to be worth anything, has to be the result of striving, of realising that we might not succeed and of overcoming an obstacle so that 'I can't' becomes 'I can and I did'. To win you have to dare to lose. When success comes too easily children can suffer, as do many child stars and models, whose success is not of their own doing; it comes because they look right and have parents who are willing to ferry them to auditions. When they lose those advantages and find themselves passed over, they are unprepared for the feelings of frustration and failure.

One reason why few children stick at anything long enough to do really well is that so many options are open to them. When they hit an obstacle, rather than overcome it, they move on to another activity. And parents let them. Many parents seem to consider children fragile, when, in fact, they are more resilient than adults because they worry less about what others will think of them.

Of course, parents should protect children from unbroken failure. But if given the confidence to cope with setbacks, children can gain from the character-building experiences of temporary failure. Defeats, after all, are more common than victories, so it is all the more important for children to get used to handling them positively, to see them as honourable and constructive rather than humiliating.

A dancer may find she grows too tall or loses the spark that made her special. She has to be able to get back on her feet and try something new, converting the value of what she has learnt to some fresh aim. A good attitude to failure can spur a child on to try harder next time, maybe in a different field. One child chess star who had top ranking aged twelve, but then started to lose, went on to run a computer games company, having learnt that he had to make sacrifices to succeed.

## Why competitive activities are good for a child

Chess coach Bilal Ghafoor used to love competitions when he was younger, although he didn't often win them. 'I remember thinking that it was the only area of my whole life where I had complete control,' he says. 'There was no luck involved. How well or badly I did came entirely from my own actions.'

For his pupils now he sets up competitions – with prizes not just for the winner, but also for the most improved players. In schools he finds his pupils enjoy competition. Outside school he finds they are more worried by it. 'Girls don't seem to mind so much,' he says, 'but boys can be suicidal when they lose. I've seen some children so upset that they have sworn not to play ever again. Mostly that's the fault of the parents. They put too much pressure on them when they should be teaching them that losing doesn't matter.

'I've seen situations where parents have been heartbroken that Johnny has had a few bad scores. Even if parents aren't pressurising children at that moment, it's in the ethos of the household: we must win, we must get a bigger house or all is lost . . .

'But there are also some supportive parents whose kids get upset. I tell those kids that they have to learn that losing is not that bad if they feel they have done reasonably well. "If you go in expecting to lose every game," I tell them, "every win will be a bonus. Or, if you lose in this tournament, next year you can see if you can do better." Like anything in life, you can learn from failure, or be destroyed by it.'

## Can parents help children cope with winning and losing?

I talked to Noël about what parents could do to help their children cope with success and failure. She believes it is an area in which training is vital, and that parents can train both competitive and reluctant children to take the ups and downs of life in their stride, to realise that success comes from taking lots of little steps in the right direction, to be prepared to make mistakes and to learn from failures.

'What you want,' she said, 'is a child who can enjoy competition without letting it colour his life, who is content to compete without resorting to dirty tricks. You want a child to compete because children are much more confident when they are stretching themselves, when they feel they've accomplished something. That zest for achievement, that urge to strive for highs is built into human nature, and those who don't get it in any other way often resort to drugs or drink to provide alternative highs.'

I asked her whether she felt that parents' only choice was, as Paula Yates once put it, between bringing up 'anxious achievers or happy blobs'. She didn't agree. 'There are children,' Noël said, 'who are confident enough to say, "I didn't do my best" or "Even though I won, it was only because the other player was weak". Such children can be naturally modest because they aren't living and breathing the need to win.

'To some this balance seems to come naturally because they have a laid-back temperament, but other children can be taught and trained to take competition in their stride.'

In her view, attitudes to success and failure all come down to fear of both winning and losing, and parents can equip all types of children for both outcomes.

We talked about the various types of child and how they can be helped.

## The uncompetitive child

Easygoing, laid-back children are often uninterested in competition. If such a child wants to take part in a sport that is competitive, the parents will have to work out how to motivate her. How you help depends on the child's nature. A child who is not naturally a team player may not try her best or be physically assertive, since the point of the game is not important to her; she may need a solo activity. When, however, you have a child who doesn't like doing things alone and doesn't feel the need to overcome an opponent, that child may find it easier to focus on winning if she is part of a team.

## The over-competitive child

This is a more common problem. The child doesn't understand that you can enjoy something even when it is not going your way. Often parents are irritated by the child's reaction to losing and say, 'Lump it' in an annoyed way, which doesn't help. The child feels criticised on top of feeling that he has failed.

The parents may have exacerbated their child's competitive streak by trying to make sure he doesn't fail.

Perhaps the child is always comparing himself to others; this may not be the parents' fault. They may have been scrupulous about not comparing their child to other children, but still have a naturally competitive child.

## The bad loser

This child gets angry with the winner, and possibly also with the coach and the judge. She is looking for someone or something to blame – bad luck, perhaps – rather than looking at her own performance. Some kids whine and whinge about 'the wind' or 'not feeling well', or say their grip is slippery. The child may even lie or cheat to win, and become upset, grumpy or annoyed for a long time after losing or not doing well. She cannot be honest with herself and say, 'I didn't kick that well. I could do it better.'

The child catastrophises – expects the worst – or sees the glass as half empty, and in doing so she convinces herself that everything is going wrong. She is unrealistic, believing herself to be more talented or skilled than she really is. She judges her self-worth by winning or coming close to the top, and sees any mistake as a character defect instead of an event to learn from.

## The bad winner

This child is too competitive. He boasts or shows off, and displays arrogance or contempt for those who aren't as good at the activity as he is. This child believes it says something very significant about him if he wins, that he is a good person. Of course, if he loses, he thinks he is a bad person. This child is very self-absorbed, so lacks sensitivity about how losers may be feeling because he has immature social skills and is not yet able to empathise with others.

## The perfectionist

This type of child may be talented but not confident, and would often rather not attempt something unless she is sure of doing well. She gives up quickly – as soon as she feels she is not doing well, or something has gone wrong. She is unrealistic because she does not know her own strengths and cannot admit her own mistakes. She may think it is necessary to be perfect immediately. She may not realise that the point of learning is to get better. She can be rude and aggressive, irritable and impatient, as she feels bound to fail. The child may switch off and be unwilling to try, or may be rushed or disorganised.

## The big-head

Big-headedness doesn't come from success; it comes from a mixture of the child's temperament and the way the parents handle his competitiveness. It's about always seeing things in relation to others, sniping at them, saying 'I'm better than you are' or 'That's easy'. When children boast it is almost always because they feel not as good as they might be. Often lurking in the background are parents who worry that their child is not confident enough, so they say, 'Marvellous' and 'Brilliant' to try to encourage him. This makes the child unrealistic about his own abilities. Descriptive praise about a child's actual achievements –

'That hand looks very lifelike' – is less likely than evaluative praise of the 'brilliant' variety to lead a child to overestimate his own talents.

## How do you persuade an uncompetitive child to compete?

The child who doesn't want to take part because he is frightened of losing is often, Noël finds, a naturally intense and anxious child, who feels things in a heightened way. He may think that his parents will be upset – or even not love him – if he doesn't succeed. He may also, because of his temperament, have learnt to get attention by being helpless.

'Sensitive, intense children,' she says, 'get a lot of molly-coddling. People tiptoe around their negative feelings. Then, every now and then, the parents snap and lecture the child about what he should be feeling and doing. This pendulum effect only makes the child more sensitive and intense.

'This child needs to be put into situations where he will lose so that he can get used to it. You need to prepare the child by saying that at first it is going to feel quite hard to lose. Soon the child will realise that he has survived not winning or not reaching the score he wanted.'

A child who cannot bear the thought of competition may fear he will be very upset if he loses but he is usually worried that the outcome matters too much to a parent. If the parent suspects this is the case, she will need to listen reflectively to the child's feelings, talk about all the different ways a match could go, and show, rather than simply say, that all she wants is for her child to do his best. It is important for the child to visualise winning, but even more important to visualise doing his best and maybe not winning. Experienced athletes don't visualise collecting the medals; they focus on doing their best, realising that they can't predict the result, as someone else may run the race even faster.

It may also be that the child is not yet mature enough to

handle the ups and downs of a highly competitive sport. Perhaps he needs to try a less competitive activity that will develop his social skills, possibly a team activity, where he need not worry so much about his individual performance.

## Overcoming fear of success

The child who doesn't want to compete in case he wins may have got the impression that it is bad to be talented or ambitious. 'In Britain there is a fear of being a tall poppy, of sticking out from the crowd, or being thought "up yourself",' says Noël. 'The child may have experienced, or may assume, that other children will resent him if he is better at something than they are, or think him big-headed or a show-off. He may fear that they will not want to be his friend if he is a star, or that they will want him to fail.

'He may not realise that what people react badly to is not his success, but his showing off. He may think others dislike him, when the problem is that he doesn't understand about encouraging others and not showing off, and so makes others feel frustrated and annoyed. The parent will then have to train the child in more mature social skills.

'Possibly, the sensitive, intense, impulsive child may not realise that he doesn't have to feel in competition with others. Again, the parent needs to explore the child's fears through reflective listening. It may be that he has heard classmates make horrible remarks about him. Parents are quick to point out that those children were not his real friends, but the child feels hurt nonetheless. Lecturing doesn't help. Over time, with descriptive praise, reflective listening and reliable routines, the child can learn to cooperate with others and "compete with himself", accepting that sometimes he will learn faster than others, and sometimes more slowly, but that the idea is to keep learning and improving.

'Another reason why a child may not want to compete is that he fears if he wins once, he may always be expected to win. Parents need to show that child that it is terrific to win once.

Reflective listening to the child's fears will help him understand that you don't expect too much.'

She adds a word of warning: 'Reflective listening is not a quick fix. Such conversations aren't a one-off; they go on over months and years, but they are far more effective than a lecture.'

## What do you do with a child who is too competitive?

According to Noël, 'Children will always want to win, especially intense children for whom everything really matters. There's nothing wrong in that, but the parent needs to change the child's focus so that he learns to compete against himself. That will require hard work, not wishy-washy bits of advice about not comparing yourself.'

Many children are so desperate to win that they lie, cheat, try to bend the rules, make nasty comments about the other players and argue with the referee. Perhaps they learn this behaviour from watching some of the more show-off professionals: some children seem to be under the impression that to do well at something, to gain respect – and to scare the opposition – you have to have 'attitude'.

Often, though, it is the fault of a parent making a child feel under too much pressure to succeed. One girl on the tennis circuit was known as 'the cheat of Middlesex'. She got that way because her father didn't let her have dinner if she lost. Eventually she gave up the game.

In tennis, where children are often left to decide between themselves who won a point, some try barefaced whoppers about line judgements. 'My daughter is more calm and composed than most of them,' says a tennis father. 'I've seen her opponents scream, throw their rackets, cheat and lie, and I've trained my daughter to go and shake their hands. She says to me: "Daddy, I've tried my best," and then we discuss what she might have done differently.

'She's younger than many of the people she is playing, which makes them even more determined not to be beaten by her, and more willing to cheat to do so. She knows that at her age she is never going to beat everyone. At the moment I am trying to teach her to stand up for herself and say when she thinks it was her point.'

It is often difficult for children in competitive sports because their friends are the people they see all the time at the club. Then, when it comes to a race, they have to switch and see them as competitors. It is not impossible to do both. 'A lot of my friends are in running,' says a teenage athlete. 'When it's a race, you are out for yourself. Then, as soon as you are off the tracks, you are friends again.'

Often the skill a child needs to learn to make that happen is how to praise others, not in an evaluative or grovelling way, which is often embarrassing – 'You were fantastic, so much better than me' – but realistically: 'You really get off the blocks fast.'

Noël's advice is: 'Make clear before each session the behaviour required, and afterwards give feedback using descriptive praise. "It was really mature that you didn't show how upset you were when the other side got that goal . . ." etc.'

## What do you do about a child who turns against his team members when they lose?

The child might say: 'We would have won if Joe hadn't fumbled the ball.' Even though the coach explains that it was Joe this time, but it could have been anyone, the child still goes on about the boy who lost the match. The coach finds this exasperating and Joe feels humiliated.

'This child clearly had assumed that his team would win,' says Noël, 'and is upset that the unthinkable happened. Before the next match the parent has to help the child imagine the possibility of losing the match. One way is for the parent to listen reflectively *many times* to the child's feelings. This doesn't mean agreeing with the child about Joe, nor does it mean saying, "You are really angry with Joe . . ." because the child's feelings go much deeper than that. Whenever the child starts saying something unpleasant about a team member, stop what you are doing and use reflective listening to help the child understand what he really is feeling.

'This is more effective in stopping such remarks than saying something like, "I won't tolerate that kind of talk", which stops it termporarily at best. You must show you aren't tolerating it by insisting that the child take a more thoughtful line and rephrase his sentiments, then and there.'

## How to stop a child becoming a perfectionist

The drive to perfectionism crops up regularly in accounts of adolescents with eating disorders. According to researcher Dr Suniya Luthar of Columbia University, 'Often these children have parents who refuse to see them as they really are, who treat them as extensions of their own bloated egos.'

Hot-housing (which means pushing a child so far so fast that he has little time to enjoy other activities) can cause a lack of creativity, she also found, and a degree of self-criticism that can develop into full-scale depression. But the answer, her research suggests, is not to expect little of children, but to spend time with them. Those who fared worst in Dr Luthar's study were often home alone, whereas those who negotiated the competitive culture best were those whose parents were around when they needed to talk to them. Their parents weren't too critical, they praised the things the children did well and focused on helping them improve.

Perfectionism is a form of vanity, an unrealistic belief in yourself. 'Without ever having been spoilt by their parents,' Noël says, 'intense children want things their way; they are sensitive and little things matter to them. They can easily become perfectionists. Parents have to consciously hold back and *not* make things all right for these children so they get used to having a good time even when things are not perfect.'

## How do you stop a child appearing big-headed?

Children who can do something well are often considered big-headed. Noël suggests teaching children the difference between 'showing' and 'showing off'. They will arouse less envy and resentment if they keep quiet about a skill and let others notice that they swim like a fish or sing like an angel when the moment arises naturally. That way the child will also avoid the embarrassment of saying he can do something and then, perhaps, not managing to pull it off and looking a fool.

'Children are impulsive,' says Noël, 'and usually can't wait for someone to notice their talent. A parent can anticipate that by saying that of course they want people to notice how good they are. They can discuss when an opportunity might arise in the near future.

'Parents can also train their children in the convention that applies when some other child says she can't do something. The child who responds by saying, "Oh, but *I* can," will look like a bighead. The correct response is to encourage the other person, who may then ask the child if he knows how to do it. The child can then admit that he does and demonstrate whatever it is without appearing big-headed.

## How do you teach a child to be a team player?

To some it comes naturally; to others it doesn't, which is all the more reason to train children by putting them in for some team activities.

'Beforehand,' Noël suggests, 'you should talk through with the child what is involved in being part of a team. You could discuss and practise with the child the simple social skills of greeting, making eye contact, smiling.

'Then move on to the more complex skills involved in being part of a team: giving feedback, complimenting others (many children are not willing to do that), encouraging and cheering up other players, not laughing at them.

'Other useful skills are those that help a child build a relationship with the coach. You could explain to the child that these will stand her in good stead. They include: joining in with unloading, finding missing objects, clearing up. The child might not have realised that those who are playing about or standing around are more likely to get shouted at. Unconsciously, the coach will deem them to be spoilt brats and will think: "Do they think I'm their servant?"'

---

**HOW TO TEACH A CHILD SPORTSMANSHIP**
The child may be a bad winner, a bad loser or a perfectionist because he has not yet understood adult values. You want a child to enjoy competition and the thrill of the game, to throw himself into it without feeling that it is a matter of life and death. That means learning sportsmanship. This consists of:

- Sharing opportunities and glory.
- Seeing that competition is not the most important thing.
- Feeling and showing respect and consideration.
- Honesty.

- Get the child to anticipate and role-play how he might feel if he had just won or just been beaten, and what would be a sensible way to behave as compared to a way that would alienate others.
- Get him into the habit of saying something positive about team-mates and the opposition (or what the child sees as the opposition). These should not be general statements, such as, 'They were very good', but exactly what made them better players or a better team. It will take training, rather than pleading, to instil this habit, as the child who loves to win also hates to lose.

---

- Then get the child to say some of those positive things to the team-mates or opposition. One father trained his child to do this by insisting that after every game he played with his son, they each had to compliment the other.
- Keep the child stretched. A child who is indeed very gifted won't have the feeling that what matters most is being better than someone else if she is always competing against herself, striving to do better.
- Help the child analyse her own mistakes. You could point out that those who are able to be honest about their own performance are more likely to win next time.

## The psychological aspects of a game

A good coach will not just teach technical skills, such as how to kick a rugby ball like Jonny Wilkinson. He will also give guidance on the psychological aspects of the game that allow or prevent children from doing their best. Sion Thomas, a sports psychologist who coaches the GB Tennis Girls team of young players, has experience of a range of other sports that he draws on in his work on mental attitude.

Like all coaches, he believes that 'if you fail to prepare, you prepare to fail'. His preparations cover physical techniques, such as deep breathing and practising. He also helps players to set achievable goals for themselves, and does behavioural and cognitive work: 'This is about developing habits and pre-performance routines to cope with the moments of irrationality that you get in all sports.'

One area he focuses on is concentration cues – words or mental images that help a player to stay in the present rather than to be worrying about the last point, which is history, or the unknowable end result. 'Players who chastise themselves for an error or a missed goal become over-aware of the next point,' he says. 'Many players' biggest enemy is themselves. They get so taken up with their thoughts that they don't notice what is happening in the game. They worry too much about making mistakes.

'A player who can stay in the present is at a great advantage. Serena Williams, for example, made forty-seven unforced errors in a Wimbledon final. At that point most people would have generalised the mistakes and decided that everything was going wrong. But she had the mental discipline not to worry about the mistakes – and went on to win the match. Golfers too have to give themselves permission to miss the fairway a certain amount of the time.'

He spends time working with players on the tendency to negative self-talk, such as: 'She's ranked higher, I won't win.' For every negative remark going through her head, he asks the player to think up a positive one. So instead of thinking, 'I missed that ball,' they learn to say instead, 'I was in a good position, I just needed to be a bit further forward.'

As background, he gets them to write a performance profile of themselves, giving themselves marks out of ten against a number of criteria. When he then compares these with coaches' opinions he finds they often underrate themselves. Realism is vital to success, so he gets players to look at the way they express themselves. When a player throws down a racket in frustration and says, 'I can't serve today,' he gets them to realise that what they actually mean is: 'I am having difficulty serving today.'

'I want players to develop an awareness,' he says, 'of how thought affects feelings, and how feelings affect behaviour.'

Following on from that, he discusses with the players the ways in which they avoid taking responsibility for their own performance when something goes wrong. It is common to blame the umpire or say, 'It wasn't my fault' or 'I never play well when I'm nervous'. Those he coaches have to learn what they can't control – which might be the power of the opponent's serve or the weather – and what they can. Self-awareness helps them to accept responsibility for what happens on court, and improves their game.

'But there is only so much I can do to prepare players for success,' he says. 'It is what happens outside the lessons that matters most.' Again, this is down to the parents.

## Should a parent let a child win?

It is delightful to see the pleasure on a child's face when he or she wins over a parent. Mine dance round the room in triumph, and I am tempted to lose to them deliberately so that they can enjoy another bout of such joy. However, I also know that it is important for parents to prepare children for defeats to come.

'The child who is allowed to win at home, perhaps because she's the youngest,' says Noël, 'will be at a disadvantage in the outside world, where others will not let her win; then she will feel confused and unhappy.

'Parents should never deliberately lose to a child. If the child realises that is what the parent is doing, then there is no challenge. If the child doesn't realise, he will think the parent is pathetic. Instead, you can play games where skill is not involved so that the child has an equal chance of winning. When you are playing a game of skill, openly give yourself a handicap so you aren't unrealistically inflating the child's ego.'

The father of Magnus Carlsen, who became a chess grand-master aged twelve, was his first teacher. He didn't want to play deliberately badly against his son when he was very young, as that would have been teaching him the wrong moves, so at first he would play with only pawns and do his best to beat his son, who had a full set of pieces. By the time his son was eight or nine, the boy was beating him every time, however hard he tried, but he kept on playing him occasionally – for a very good reason. 'I could not learn chess from my father,' Magnus says, 'but I did learn from him how to lose with grace.'

## Are exams a good idea?

No teacher should put a child in for an exam that he is likely to fail. Exams are a good way to keep a child looking ahead and trying more difficult things. From the parents' point of view, they are also useful ways of seeing whether the teacher is any good: someone whose pupils all get 'honours' is clearly doing a good job.

Michael Crookes, a ballet examiner, was able to explain some further uses of exams. 'When I was six,' he said, 'I didn't see the point of learning cold syllabus exercises. Only later did I come to see that exams were vital to the gradual increase, at a safe pace, of my dance vocabulary. An examiner is trained not just to assess a child's standard, but the faults that could result in injury.

'From the endless purgatory of repeating exercises I developed a muscle memory, a polished technique and the assurance to let my creative side shine. I also learnt grooming (vital for auditioning later), being early, and courtesy towards fellow dancers.'

---

**TIPS FOR HELPING CHILDREN WITH EXAMS**
Assuming that the teacher has done his part, the parent should:
- Arrange for the child to play/dance/sing to numerous strangers before the exam to get over the worst nerves.
- Give the child a proper meal beforehand.
- Give a morale boost in the form of a new book or item of clothing.
- Leave early.
- Bring water.
- Bring spares and music (or whatever equipment is required).

---

## Should you let children skip exams?

One of my daughters came out howling from Grade 1 piano. She found the combination of a strange room and not one, but two, silent examiners (a trainee was sitting in) so terrifying that she lost her way repeatedly and emerged eager to give up the instrument rather than ever have to face such an experience again.

I asked Noël whether I should let her off further exams. 'You don't want to leave it up to her, and you don't want to overreact and say something you will regret later,' she replied. 'You could say, "Daddy and I have decided that you won't do another exam until you are happy about it." You could postpone the next exam by a year, but let her move on to new, more difficult pieces. There is no point in her doing the exam if she is too anxious to do her best. Parents can help children become less anxious through using the sixteen skills [see *How to Be a Better Parent*].'

Another daughter described her terror of doing Grade 1 violin as 'like standing on the top of a very high mountain'. Again I feared the worst, but she survived it, and when she learnt she had passed she seemed to grow up before my eyes. It gave her tremendous confidence to know that she had applied herself to something she found hard and succeeded. The next day she even practised voluntarily.

Of course a child is likely to be much more anxious about exams if the parent appears to care more about the result than about whether the child enjoys learning the instrument.

## How to get a child through an audition

Preparation is the key. Take a relaxed attitude: maybe you will get in, maybe you won't, but it's always worth a try. Remind children that people are chosen for roles for many reasons, not always because of their talent. Girls in shows are often chosen to match the boys, who are harder to find; height and hair colour may be crucial. (At my audition for the National Youth Theatre I was told not to assume any talent if I was picked as they also chose people for being 'nice to have around' and 'because we feel sorry for them'.)

As the child goes into the audition, it is not a good idea to say: 'Do your best'. If it doesn't work out, the child will think his best is worthless. 'Enjoy it' is better.

Another lesson that I have learnt only after getting it wrong several times is not to deluge a child with questions as soon as she comes out of the audition. Lucille Bryants, who auditions children for the London Children's Ballet, often cringes as she hears parents launch into a cross-examination. '"How did it go?" they demand, "What did you do?" and always, always, "What were the others like?"

'I've seen children destroyed,' she says, 'by having their mothers always comparing them, viewing everyone else as competition, always looking for approval from others and making crushing remarks when the child fails, such as: "Oh well, you obviously didn't try hard enough." That's pretty damaging for a child who is already trying to deal with her own disappointment.'

---

**WHAT'S PUSHY?**

- Parents who use the vocabulary of winning and losing about trivial things, such as who got somewhere first or who got the most presents.
- Parents who boast about a child's victories.
- Parents who want children to achieve on several fronts at once.
- Parents who hold grudges.
- Parents who barge into rehearsals and complain that their child hasn't been given a part.
- Parents who question the referee's and linesman's decisions, and who think they are the best judges of a child's talent.
- Parents who think supporting involves booing the opponents.
- Parents who are in a hurry. It matters more if the child is still playing a sport aged sixteen, than if he is in the first eleven at the age of twelve.

---

# 6

## A QUESTION OF PRACTICE

How do I get a child to practise?
How often should a child practise?
What do I do if he doesn't want to?
How to structure a good practice session.

Getting a child to practise can be the bane of a would-be positive parent's life. I can't bear to think how many ugly scenes in my household have run along the following lines.

**Me:** Have you done your violin practice?
**Child:** No.
**Me:** Well, do it now.
[Child groans, moans, disappears. Reappears ten minutes later with instrument.]
**Me:** I've only got fifteen minutes before I make dinner, so get on with it now.
**Child:** All right, then.
[A small amount of half-hearted scraping at the violin then ensues and I get increasingly irritated.]
**Me:** Why don't you just do it properly?
[Child slams down violin and walks off.]
**Me:** Well, no television for you, then, until you've finished.
**Child:** Waaaah . . .

At times the foregoing scenario has left everyone so wound up and miserable that I have felt like telling the child to give up the instrument. I don't, of course, because I have invested so much time and money in finding a good teacher, buying the violin, taking the child to lessons and so forth. I also have a vision of the child a few years on enjoying being part of an orchestra or playing alone when she feels low, so I persevere. But I often think, 'What's the point?' and so, no doubt, does the child.

While most children know that doing their homework is not negotiable, and that they will get into trouble at school if they fail to do it, practising extra-curricular activities doesn't seem such a clear-cut duty. And, because children feel practising is negotiable, it becomes a wonderful way to wind up parents.

Some parents, however, seem to manage better than me. At one low point I spoke to a mother of two sons, who have both won music scholarships to desirable schools. 'They must be amazingly gifted,' I said, but she wouldn't accept that description. They had worked hard at it and done their practice every day. Both had reached Grade 8 by the age of thirteen, which strikes me as phenomenal. And this woman works outside of the home. How on earth had she got them to practise? 'You've got to make it such an ingrained habit that it is like brushing their teeth every day – just something they do, something that they don't even think about. I don't have to tell them now.'

## What is the point of practice?

Practising is not just a way to inflict torture on parents and children: it is essential, not just in music, but in every activity, for transferring the skills learnt in a weekly lesson from the conscious to the subconscious mind, and from the short-term memory to the long-term memory. That leaves the conscious mind uncluttered and ready for the next bit of learning. This only happens if you practise often enough for the new bit of learning to become automatic – and that means not just one quick practice before the lesson to show willing, but several times a week, preferably daily.

The point of practice is only rarely to make perfect; the usual point is to make progress, which is motivating. Unless a child has mastered a new skill between one lesson and the next, you are wasting your money, the teacher will soon feel that he or she is wasting his or her time, and the child will feel discouraged. She will then drop the activity, so practice must be done.

This doesn't mean that children can be expected to realise how important it is to practise. As a man in charge of training at the Football Association told me: 'All children think they can be Wayne Rooney simply by watching him on television. Good players make a game look easy. The child can spot mistakes, but he doesn't know how many hours Rooney put in as a child honing his skills while his friends were goofing around.'

Children take up an activity, whether it is a sport or an instrument, because it looks like fun. They don't understand about hard work, especially when they are young. So a child can't just 'get on with it' – as I have often foolishly, pointlessly, instructed my children. Every parent of a successful child has had to make practice happen by thinking through what is involved, making the rules plain, and understanding what it is about practising that children find unpleasant and difficult.

Noël advises that parents shouldn't put practising in a category of its own, but should consider it just another aspect of the training that we owe our children in order to help them acquire the skills that will stand them in good stead in later life, and the habits that will help them become all that they could one day be.

When it comes to homework, we know it makes sense. Unless you practise the sums at home that you have learnt to do in class, the mathematical techniques won't become fixed in the mind. Homework, at least, is something we all sign up for with the home/school agreement that we are given when children start primary school. It comes in neat packages – this page, this exercise, this worksheet – so you can see what's required and when it will come to an end. That isn't to say it is always easy to get children to do their homework. (For tips on that see Chapter 10 in *How to Be a Better Parent*.) Practising is more nebulous than homework, but just as essential.

A Suzuki violin teacher with thirty years' experience, who has children aged seven or eight taking Grade 5 exams, says she can tell soon after they start lessons which children will go far: 'They are the ones who put the work in; the ones with the parents who help them. Those who drop out are the ones who don't have time for regular practice.'

Yet, although most of us have few qualms about setting aside a patch of the evening for homework, we are more chaotic about dedicating time to practising other activities – and that is why it becomes a battleground. Because we are dealing with optional activities, such as sport and music, that a child has usually chosen to do, we believe that the practice should be fun, a pleasure in itself rather than a means to an end. We find it harder to lay down the law about practising to a child who is resistant, so we make excuses and let him off. Or we allow ourselves to be drawn into pointless arguments and negotiations, which end up eroding our authority even further.

Practice, even more than homework, tends to take place during time that adults consider their own, so again we aren't as firm as we might be about making it happen because we don't want a scene. Then, of course, the child gets the impression that practice isn't essential, and the problems start. When I told Noël that I sometimes ducked practice to avoid the battles she said: 'I know I may sound like an insufferable prig, but there don't have to be battles if you handle practising properly.'

## Some reasons why children hate practising

- Practising can seem lonely. Small children rarely want to be alone, so the parent (or a substitute) has to be there, making it happen and providing encouragement.
- Children live in the moment; they don't have the maturity to take a long view. All they are aware of is that someone is watching television, if not in their own home, then somewhere in the universe, and that, while they are practising, they aren't that someone. So they need a parent – preferably two – to get

them cracking, to provide the structure and enthusiasm that they usually lack.
• Children associate practising with parents being impatient with them, so it becomes something they dread.

## At what age can a child be expected to practise?

Children practise skills naturally and all the time from an early age. They fit boxes into one another, plait dolls' hair and sing along to their favourite tunes. That kind of practise doesn't seem like hard work, and children quickly master those skills.

Whether a child will put the same effort into practising skills that are harder to master and not so immediately rewarding depends both on the child's temperament and on the rewards that flow from the practice. Some children instantly recognise something that they will come to love. Violinist Tamsin Little was given her first violin when she was scarcely more than a toddler, and from the moment it was placed in her hands she took it everywhere and played it all the time. No parental pressure was required to get her to practise. And, of course, when she quickly became very good, she felt successful, so she had every reason to carry on.

Teachers who use the Suzuki method to teach a variety of instruments, not only violin and piano, often start children very young. I asked Clare Santer, a Suzuki teacher, whether they could be expected to practise at the age of two or three. 'The advantage of starting children very young, before they start school,' she said, 'is that you can let them have several mini-practices in a day, rather than one long one.'

Knowing how hard it can be for parents to supervise, she teaches the parents how to do it properly. If the parent knows how to sit at the piano or hold the bow correctly, the child learns through imitation and osmosis.

Where a parent doesn't have time for all that Santer wouldn't bother to start a child learning an instrument at a very early age. The youngest at which she said children could be expected to practise on their own was seven or eight. 'Leave it until the child is old enough to supervise himself,' she says. 'Many children have done well from a late start. They are more physically adept and have heard more music.'

## So how do you get children to practise?

I have one child who has to be prevented from practising music non-stop (the same does not go for homework), and another child who doesn't need to be asked, although she is by no means obsessed. But most of my children find practising a chore and manage to get away with less practice than they need. Then, because progress is slow, they feel cack-handed and frustrated. To get them to do it I have to be on hand providing masses of descriptive praise when they so much as take the instrument out of its case.

Giving children the feeling that they can earn parental approval by practising certainly helps motivate them, but on its own it has not been enough. Rules, routines and rewards are also necessary, as are talk-throughs, the teaching of microskills and dividing difficult pieces into more manageable, bite-sized chunks. I went back to the mother of the two children with music scholarships for advice. She herself had studied music at university, and still plays, although her work is unrelated to music. To her, learning a musical instrument is vital; to her husband, who doesn't play an instrument himself, it is an optional extra. However, he agreed with her about practising, so they were able to present a united front, and every morning before school the children have played their two instruments apiece.

'It has taken a long time,' she admitted, 'to get the boys to the stage where they treat practising as a normal part of daily life. I used to be the one to practise with them because I know how to tune the violin and I can tell when they are doing it wrong. But I can't always be there. At those times it is better that my husband listens to them than that they try and do it on their own, just as it is more important that they get the instrument out and do some practice than that the practice is done brilliantly.

'I know I can be a hard taskmaster, but as they have got older, I have learnt to back off and let them do it themselves. When the children play I don't correct them. I leave correction to the teacher, except just before an exam, when I will tell them if something is wrong.'

---

**SUZUKI TIPS FOR HAPPIER PRACTISING**
- Don't give a child a cold room for practising.
- Know what they've got to practise and in what order.
- Never work on more than one thing that needs improvement in a practice session.
- Children are very good critics of themselves. Let the child judge when something is good enough.
- Play tapes of the music often so that the child knows how a piece should sound.
- Chart progress.
- Vary the order.
- Wear silly hats.
- Work towards a performance at the end of the week. Choose three pieces to perform. Envisage the performance as a meal with starter, main course and pudding.

---

## How to structure a successful practice session

A small amount of frequent practice is far more effective than a few long, irregular sessions. 'Before learning new material,' says Noel, 'we need to bring the previously practised skills to the front of the child's mind so that he can focus and think about them. The way to do this is always to start each session with really easy pieces or steps or skills. It may seem like a waste of time, but it helps confidence and it prepares the brain and the eye-hand co-ordination for more difficult skills so that the child doesn't make so many mistakes.

Don't rush this first stage. Most of the practice time should then be spent on skills or work of medium-level difficulty. Many music teachers give children quite difficult pieces, which don't bring much satisfaction to the children as they realise they are making a lot of mistakes. Spend only a few minutes of each practice session on hard or new skills. If the child is having trouble, break down each difficult area into its component parts.

Many coaches and teachers expect children to pick up where they left off last week, and are impatient if they can't. 'Learning,' says Noël, 'is always two steps forward (understanding) and one step back (as some of what was learnt falls out of the short-term memory).

Unless practising frequently, a child will forget, and won't cope physically or mentally. She warns: 'Even if the child does practise regularly, it is usual to find that some of the skills learnt in the last lesson have been forgotten. Any teacher should accept that and begin each lesson by going over what should have been learnt and revising as necessary.

'Some teachers dot around rather than revising previously learnt skills each time, and children end up forgetting a lot. Then they feel useless and think they are getting worse rather than better. When you are alerting the teacher to this problem, don't say in front of your child: "He forgets easily" – that is a form of unintentional programming. It would be better to say "Everyone forgets . . ." or, if you want to keep it personal, "My child learns best through repetition [which is universally true], so could he have a little time at the beginning of each lesson to practise the earlier skills?" You must be emphatic that this is what your child needs. Otherwise the teacher may say other children aren't having this problem.

'Increase practice gradually in frequency, duration and intensity.'

## Practise under a variety of conditions

The more different ways in which a child practises something, the more solidly she will remember it and the better she will learn to cope with new situations. So when teaching a child to catch a ball, for example, do it straightforwardly at first, then move further away or use a smaller ball. 'One father,' says Noël, 'played ball-games with his son in semi-darkness so that the child learnt to gauge where the ball was from the father's body movements, and eventually could assess direction, strength, spin and so on.

'One great way to introduce variety is to make a child practise while he is distracted. When the child first starts to learn a skill, we try to remove all distractions. But to achieve automaticity, we need to reintroduce distractions later. It could be humming while the child is playing. One mother tickled her daughter's arms while she was playing her scales so that she could learn to play under any conditions.'

## Let the child set the goals

Ask a child before every practice what he wants to achieve, Noël suggests. 'The child gets to set his own targets. That is good both for talented players and for those who aren't outstanding: it teaches a child to judge his own performance realistically, instead of being too optimistic or pessimistic.

'Help the child track or evaluate his performance in practice sessions. This could be a matter of spotting the percentage success by saying, for example, "You got the ball in the net 20 per cent of the time," or "You played it four times before it was perfect."'

## Visualise

It is possible to improve a skill that can't be practised at home by simply visualising. This is also useful with activities that parents are often too busy to take children to do mid-week, such as skating. 'When done properly,' Noël says, 'visualising can have the same effect on the neural pathways as actually doing the activity.'

It worked for Noël, who, as a child, fell in love with skating. 'The first time I tried I was awful,' she says. 'Then I read that you had to bend your knees. I imagined myself doing so, and the next time I was a million times better. My mind had been practising and so sent my knees the right message.'

Visualisation is a technique that professional coaches also use. Dr David Smith, a lecturer and researcher in sports psychology at Chester College, teaches it to golfers and athletes. 'To be really effective,' he says, 'visualisation has to engage all your senses. There is no point lying around thinking about a trip to the gym as though you were watching. Feel what it's like to be there, smell it, hear the noises.'

## Give tiny bits of advice

Use simple phrases, such as 'Wrist up', not 'You really must keep your wrists up because . . .' (a nag). Demonstrating is not enough. Explain cause and effect and help the child to work out why he is doing something wrong. For example, a coach who was teaching young footballers to kick with the side of the foot found that one boy kept kicking with his toes. Rather than simply telling him it was wrong he tried to understand why the boy was doing it. 'I expect you think it goes further,' he said, 'but it doesn't. Look. Kick this one this way and this one the other way.'

It's the same principle as when a child is asked, 'What is three times two?' and replies, 'Five.' The child is much less likely to get it wrong again if, instead of saying, 'No, you idiot – six,' you say, 'Aaah, you thought you had to add.'

Or, with an ice-skating position, you can get the child to describe what should happen, and then ask her if she has got it right: 'Oh, so your foot needs to be up by your ankle,' the parent might repeat. 'Now, where is yours?'

'These are all pieces of advice that the coach or teacher may have said in passing,' Noël says, 'but not gone over often enough for the child to understand or remember. Or these may be skills that the coach has never put into words. Without encroaching on the coach's role, parents can clarify microskills that teachers and coaches haven't time to clarify, or don't realise need to be clarified.'

## Teach microskills

Microskills are the components of any major skill. So just as you can't do good handwriting if you don't know how to hold a pen, you can't hit a good shot unless you have the right grip on your racket. 'These skills need to be taught separately at first,' says Noël, 'and then children need to be taught how to blend them. Eventually they need to be able to switch from one skill or strategy to another, making quick decisions about what to use and how.'

---

**TIPS FROM PARENTS TO ENCOURAGE PRACTISING**
- Set clear rules. The child should be in no confusion about what is required. Before starting a new activity or instrument the child should know that practising will take place five days a week for however many minutes. Ideally, it should be in the same place at the same time every day, and be supervised by the same person.
- Use a timer so that there is no argument. Start the timer once the child is ready.
- Before starting each practice, the child should be rested, fed and happy.
- Mornings can work better than evenings. I found violin practice was transformed when I shifted it to after breakfast. At that time the child and I were both less tired and not so desperate to relax. It meant getting up slightly earlier, but that was better than coming home to an activity that both I and my daughter had come to dread.
- 'Don't be too rigid about practice times,' said one mother. 'It is better to do something when you have time and are in the right mood. On the other hand, try to get things done as early as possible (and out of the way) as time just drifts by.'

---

- Be there – not just in the same room absorbed in something else, but listening, commenting, encouraging, giving a child confidence, praising progress, asking interested questions about how it works, but not interfering. (I find doing a jigsaw at the same time to be perfect; it stops me staring at the child, which can make him feel uncomfortable, but doesn't absorb me totally.)
- Talk about practising. Make it a part of life, something that doesn't come as a rude surprise. Noël recommends that parents mention practising in between times, reflectively listening to a child's feelings of reluctance, but standing firm. Discuss the pieces. Or, if it is a sporting skill that is being practised, watch matches and discuss how the players are performing. Was that a good shot? Who might the player have passed the ball to?
- Let the child set goals. 'I want to serve twenty times without doing a double fault,' or 'I want to play this scale without stumbling.'
- Descriptively praise small steps in the right direction. A child may not feel like practising, but if she gets her swimming kit ready and puts it by the front door ready for the next day, you should notice and reward that behaviour with positive attention.
- Give reliable feedback. 'Many parents try to give confidence by telling children they are great at something when they are not,' said one parent. 'I think confidence comes from being honest about when they have done something well or not. To know what they are capable of, we need to spend time watching (or listening to) them practise.'
- Give irregular rewards. The occasional ice cream or new book linked to good practising is better – and easier to sustain – than star charts and suchlike.
- Video a child practising. It will motivate him if you say you will video him again when he has improved.

## How other parents have managed

One mother motivated her child to do his piano practice by putting a little gentle blame on her husband. 'Harry has been longing to show you the piece he is learning,' she chided, with the child next to her. 'I wish you would find just ten minutes to sit and listen to it.' The child, of course, had said nothing of the kind – though he probably felt it. When the father did stop everything to listen, both he and his son were delighted.

Another mother found that she was always rushed and bad-tempered when she tried to get her children to practise their instruments, so she hired a local teenager to come for an hour before school. The teenager did not have packed lunches, PE kits or clearing up after breakfast to think about, so she could give her full attention to the children. Of course, that doesn't mean you never show an interest – you can still praise a child from the next room and say you will listen when she is ready to show her mastery of a piece.

A parent of a six-year-old who is 'not particularly interested' in music says that getting the child to practise used to be 'like pulling teeth: she learnt three songs in three years'. Having checked that the pieces weren't too difficult, the mother now sits in on the practice sessions, and has found ways to make them more fun both for herself and the child. 'For example,' she says, 'I roll the dice, and my daughter has to play the piece as many times as it says. We also play a drawing game that she loves. She might draw an ice cream, then I colour in a new blob for each thing she does right – even for picking up the violin. I take the pictures to the lesson so that the teacher can see how well she has done.'

Another game that worked well when the child was younger harnessed the girl's competitive spirit. 'I made the practice like a running race,' she says. 'I would draw two lines and a finishing post. Every time she did something right I would draw her figure further along. When she didn't do something right, I would move my figure on a bit. I would always make sure she won.'

Yet another friend found a way of getting someone else to help supervise on the cheap. She paid her teenage daughter extra pocket money for supervising the younger children's music practice. It was good for the relationship between the children, good for the eldest one, who realised how much she knew, and it also meant that the teenager earned enough money to buy her own clothes (thereby removing a perennial source of parent–teenager tension).

Here's a tip for motivating children to practise. One mother taught all her children to touch-type by making it a rule that every time they wanted to play a computer game they had first to spend twenty minutes doing typing, using the Mavis Beacon software. They weren't happy about it at the time, but they are grateful now.

A mother whose child has become a top tennis player realised that practising for an hour after school every day could get boring. To make it more fun, she lined up a variety of people for him to play against. The opponents became her son's friends, and now that he is on the circuit it is much more enjoyable as he knows so many of the other players.

A mother of a gifted pianist found that, aged fourteen, her daughter decided she was too busy to keep practising. Realising that the daughter found practising by herself lonely, the mother started sitting in the practice room each day and took with her a pile of office administration – work that could be done with half her brain. The child was then happy to keep practising for a number of years. 'It might seem indulgent to keep a teenager company,' the mother said, 'but don't we all feel better doing difficult things when somebody else is with us?'

## What do I do about a child who resists practising?

'Don't attempt to reason with a child who is objecting to practising,' says Noël. 'Reasoning and explaining will just sound like nagging. The resistance stems from a feeling, not from a rational argument. The child already knows all the good reasons why he should do it, but something is getting in the way of practising becoming a habit.'

It may be, she suggests, that the rules are not clear, that violin practice, for example, is not always straight after tea on weekdays. 'Perhaps the rule is not enforced consistently. The parent may worry, quite unnecessarily, that asking the child to do something he does not want to do will destroy the child's enjoyment of the activity. Deep down the parent may believe that practising is boring, so does not enforce the rule.

'It could also be that the child feels lonely. She may not be confident or mature enough to take the initiative about practising, or to practise alone. She may not see the point of the activity, or may want to be good at whatever it is, but be impatient about the steps necessary to become good.'

In each of those cases Noël believes the parent should get back in charge of practice sessions – and supervise them. 'Watch how you talk about practice: do you make it sound like a suggestion or a requirement? Even if your words sound like a clear, definite instruction, the tone of voice you use may sound like pleading. That leads the child to think that practice is a matter of choice. Also watch your body language – by looking uncertain you may be undermining the impression you want to give of being in charge.'

## What do I do about the child who practises sloppily?

Left to their own devices, many children go through the motions of practising, but don't do their best. When they make mistakes they don't appear to notice. Nor do they show any interest in getting the details right. Such children often argue, if confronted, that the details don't matter.

'This child may be given treats too easily or too often without having to earn the goodies in his life: his pocket money, television viewing time, sleepovers,' says Noël. 'Alternatively, the skills the child has to practise may be too hard, so she feels she can never do them well enough and decides it is better not to be seen to care. The child feels under pressure and is worried about disappointing her parents. This can happen with a sensitive, intense or unconfident child, even if the parents aren't overly competitive. They may even make a point of saying that they don't care about a specific result.'

What can happen, she finds, is that a parent may believe that a child's self-esteem is dependent on being good at something. 'This can lead to a parent becoming anxious and annoyed when the child does not seem to be trying or makes careless mistakes. It seems to the parent as if the child's happiness and self-esteem are at stake.

'This can lead to effusive praise in an attempt to build confidence – "wonderful", "terrific". The child does not believe this over-the-top praise, as she can see it is not true. She may think the parent is lying. Or she may believe the parent means what he is saying, but is sadly deluded. Or the child may believe the evaluative praise and then worry that she may not be able to continue meeting her parent's expectations. Or, if the parent is very involved in this activity, the child might worry that she won't be good enough to satisfy the parent.'

One of Noël's aunts was a talented pianist, but as a teenager she learnt a safe way of rebelling against a highly critical mother. 'She later admitted that when she was angry with her mother, she would often play the wrong note deliberately, which she knew upset her mother. She would then immediately say, "Oh, sorry" – a passive-aggressive response. It was very clever. She knew her mother couldn't accuse her of outright defiance, but the girl was attempting to express her unhappiness.

'The cause of her unhappiness was not the practising, but her critical – and definitely pushy – mother, who never gave her any praise and always expected her to get better and better. She was talked of as if her musical talent was the most important thing about her. A sensitive parent in that situation would have done some reflective listening to understand the child's concerns, and become aware of the distress her criticism was causing.'

## What if homework and practising seem to clash?

Many schools, particularly independent schools, which live by their results, give even young children quite a pile of homework every night. The way to get it done is much the same as with practising: routine, a parent or parent substitute who supervises, lots of descriptive praise and a time limit. If the homework isn't done by the deadline, the parent should explain why to the teacher. A child must not spend his whole evening doing homework; children need down time to develop their imaginations, and to make their own fun and do other things, which might be playing football or practising an instrument. Exercise and the arts are just as important as academic subjects.

If a child can't get through all the homework, he may be at the wrong school or in the wrong class, or too young to cope with an outside activity that requires regular work. But when a child is motivated it is amazing what can be fitted in. A friend of one of my daughters is aiming high in swimming: she practises for an hour each morning, and three hours some evenings – and still gets her homework done.

## How do you tell when a child is overloaded?

'I wouldn't make a child practise to the point of tears like some tennis parents,' says a mother who has erected a barre in her home so that her ballet-mad children can practise. 'When my daughter says, "I don't feel like it," sometimes I let her off, but mostly I explain that if she is going to get her body to do what she wants it to do, she has to train. Children can't look into the future as adults can. Is that pushy? As a parent, you know what it's like to want to give up but, nevertheless, to keep going. Children learn that from us. The question is knowing how far to push through the pain barrier.'

There will occassionally be times when a child's enthusiasm sags because she is tired, would rather be doing something else, or the practice isn't going well. Part of the point of practising is learning to keep going during the tough times. But when a child is persistently resistant to practising, the parent has a dilemma.

Noël taught the eleven-year-old daughter of a composer. The girl had been learning three instruments. One day she turned to her mother and said that she couldn't bear the practising, so she wanted to give them all up. Her mother told her that she could drop one instrument, but that she had to keep up piano and one orchestral instrument until she was eighteen. Noël felt the parent was right to insist that the child continue with two instruments, since she believed it was so important. 'The mother's firmness,' she says, 'was far better than letting anxiety take over. She took the "if you aren't happy with it" issue out of the discussion. After all, a parent wouldn't say that about maths. Once the girl realised that music was one of the things she had to do, she relaxed. When you know that you really have to do something, paradoxically it gives you a lot of freedom.'

Another mother was faced with a difficult decision when her seven-year-old son was learning the violin. She did her best to make the half-hour a day practice enjoyable, but he was still finding it a huge chore. 'Every day we had to tick a calendar saying he had done the half-hour,' she says. 'Other parents said they sometimes cheated, but I didn't think that was right. My son was coming to hate it. He was enjoying everything else in his life – football, tennis, French, you name it – and doing his homework with no fuss, but he was developing an allergy to the violin.

'Every morning he would tell me, "My whole body is saying I hate this." I kept him doing it for a whole further year, but it was having a detrimental effect. He wasn't improving; he was learning the notes automatically and was having a hard time playing. It didn't seem right that he should have to carry on with something that was making him so miserable – even though violin is a good way to train your musical ear – so we dropped the violin.

'Instead he is doing composition on the piano with a friend, and he loves it because it feels more like mucking about and less like hard work. He can take up the violin again when he is older and can decide whether he is prepared to practise.'

Another low-stress option that many parents have suggested, if instrument practice is too much of a problem, is singing lessons. It keeps up a child's interest in music, and the practice is less onerous as the child can do it any time, anywhere – including the bathroom – and very, very few have been known to give up.

## Some other parents' views on practice dilemmas

A child who does regular swimming training was grumbling one day about going. On arriving at the pool, the parent found that she had (deliberately?) left her costume at home. Even though it was a crashing bore, he didn't make a fuss or let her skip training. He drove all the way back home, fetched the costume and insisted the child train for the rest of the time so that she didn't feel tempted to forget again.

Another mother decided differently because she could see that her management was the problem, not the practice itself. 'My daughter is an amenable girl and a doer,' she says. 'She didn't need to be nagged, but sometimes we would have terrible rows about practising. Most arose because I work full-time and have a tight schedule, so I would come home after a long day at work and shout at everyone about practice and homework they should have done in my absence. Shouting "Do it now" didn't work; nor did handing out stickers and sweeties – I'm not consistent enough to make them work, and my heart is not in them. So I would leave my daughter to fiddle around in another room, and she'd come back saying "Done" after she had been bashing away at the keys or scraping at the strings for six or seven minutes.

'Children's progress and pleasure in music is very dependent on a parent's mood! However hard one tries, children know exactly how temperamental one is feeling.'

She tried delegating the supervision of practising, but that didn't work. Rather than let the rows continue or the children give up, she has now rearranged her own life. 'Things are going better,' she says, 'since I have started attending all practice sessions. Even my elder child, who is thirteen and practises on her own, still likes me to listen and appreciate.'

'My elder son is making fast progress on the violin because he can pick out a tune quickly,' says another mother. 'My younger one is doing well on the cello. Without question, my practising with them virtually every day and being at every lesson are key to their progress. It is a huge commitment. My musical background is just sufficient – I played piano, violin and even cello briefly – to help them: the more musical the parent, and the more dedicated, the faster the child's progress.

'I am very strict. I won't allow laziness, rudeness or skiving. But as far as one can get through disciplined practice and doggedness, there comes a point where progress will stop if the child's innate musicality is insufficient. It's their love of music that sustains them through the really hard hours. If that love isn't there, or if it dries up, if they are in it for the show and not the content, then they should do different activities.'

---

**WHAT'S PUSHY?**
- Parents who come back tired from work and shout at children about the practice and homework they should have done.
- Parents who expect children always to enjoy practice.
- Parents who aren't clear about the amount of time a child is meant to practise, and ask for him to keep going beyond what is required by the teacher.
- Parents who expect practice to make perfect.

---

# 7

## THE CHILD WITH A TALENT

How do you spot a gift?
Should you let a child progress faster than the rest of his age group?
What impact can a gift have on the rest of the family?
Why don't children always seem to enjoy being talented?

When my children were tiny I was, like all other parents, keen to spot giftedness. I got wildly over-excited about quite normal achievements. This child could walk early. That one could speak very well at an early age. Was it a sign of great musicality that this one clapped along to 'The Wheels on the Bus'? Were sporting trophies likely to be filling the mantelpiece soon because my child could catch a ball?

As the children have got older, I have become wiser. The real eye-opener has been seeing truly talented children. Whenever I find myself relapsing into fond theories of latent academic or artistic genius in one of my children I remind myself of the eleven-year-old daughter of friends who composed an entertaining history of her school – in Latin – and transcribed it on to vellum in perfect calligraphy, complete with ornate initial letters that a medieval monk would have been proud of.

At times I have felt relieved that none of my children seem gifted. Gifts present parents with agonising dilemmas. If they foster the talent, they run the risk of being thought pushy. Other parents, with less gifted children, are always on the lookout for any signs of weirdness in a child who is doing extraordinary things. 'Is he a social retard? Is she doing it all to please her father?' they gossip behind the parents' backs.

Many parents, in order not to incur that criticism, play down a child's gift, keep him in a mainstream school rather than apply for scholarships, refuse to take him off to a tennis court five times a week (despite his pleas) or discourage him from entering chess tournaments for fear that he will turn out nerdy. Of course, the parents then have to worry about whether they are frustrating a child in the good cause of keeping their lives as normal as possible.

The nearest my family gets to an exceptional talent is a child who is absolutely dedicated to his guitar. From early childhood, while his siblings have wanted to try anything and everything, he has always been a serial monogamist when it comes to activities – dinosaurs, Power Rangers, Warhammer and then the guitar. While other children flit from one activity to another, and are content with competence rather than mastery, he has focused on one thing at a time. Such children see their current passion as central to their very being.

Dedicated children don't operate like others – they don't need to be kept motivated because they provide all their own motivation. The parents' worry is not how to keep them going, but how to stop them from becoming too geeky and narrow. Their single-mindedness is at once impressive and slightly worrying. As the mother of a child who loves to perform confided of her child: 'My problem is stopping her.'

Luke Scott has observed 'a fanaticism' in children and teenagers that no adult can equal as too many distractions deflect them from becoming as obsessive. 'Such children shouldn't, indeed can't, be stopped,' he says, 'but the fanatical child can present problems.' They often absorb large amounts of time and money. They beg for the next piece of equipment to support them in their drive, and require constant ferrying to competitions and coaching sessions. Parents may not want to deny them for fear of the talent drying up or the child feeling thwarted and then resenting the parent.

Some parents resist. A mother told me that she had decided not to put her sporty son in for county teams. 'We are a unified family,' she said, 'and we don't have the resources to have a genius. If I were always ferrying that boy around, I would scarcely see my other two children, and it is not worth it.'

Another mother has, however, decided that she will do any ferrying necessary to help her dance-mad children as she doesn't want to 'stand in their way'. 'Other parents think I am mad and pushy,' she says. 'It means we never go away for a weekend and I have little social life. I treat it just as I did changing their nappies when they were tiny. It is a stage that will pass very soon. By the time they are fifteen or sixteen they will be quite independent.'

How parents react to a very talented or obsessed child depends largely on their own level of talent and what they have done with it. I know families in which near-genius is taken for granted and no fuss is made over quite remarkable gifts. In such families there is often an assumption of success because the parents have themselves used their own talents.

Some families seem to live by the message behind the recent *Spiderman* film that 'Talent is not a privilege, but a responsibility. It has to be used for the good of mankind.' More often, though, they make the child think that he has a responsibility to himself to make the most of it – which is often a thinly disguised way of saying a responsibility to the parents.

The young, combat-trouser-clad opera singer Keedie Babb has parents who will stop at nothing to help their child. 'Over the years my parents have sold everything – their car, furniture, television – to help me buy costumes and equipment, and to pay for singing lessons. We have often had to eat beans on toast.' Like Beyoncé's father, such parents can never do too much for their children. As he said, 'If she had wanted to be a doctor, I would have bought her a hospital.'

As the child becomes more successful, the parents can become deeply involved. Many become their children's managers and, however good their intentions, there can be problems when the roles become blurred. If a parent has given up his job to take a child around auditions or on the chess circuit, that parent will want the child to go as far as she possibly can, even if she shows signs of flagging.

## How do you spot a real talent?

The National Association for Gifted Children finds it easy to distinguish between truly gifted children and those whom parents would like to think are gifted. When a child is really gifted the parents tend to be embarrassed, anxious and make light of the child's extraordinary achievements. They want the child to lead a normal life, whereas those who are excited by a talent are often the ones who are keen to inflate mere aptitudes into full-blown gifts.

Parents think they know their children better than anybody else does, and often they are right. That doesn't mean, however, that parents are always the most realistic judges of their children's talents. I once got very excited about one of my children's artistic talents and put him in for an art scholarship. It was a salutary experience. When we took in his portfolio of cartoons, the school's head of art looked at them with disdain, then pointed to the walls covered in vastly superior work by boys only a year older. 'The kind of boy we are looking for,' he said, 'is the one who stops the family car on holiday because he has seen a windmill he wants to sketch.' Fortunately, my son was not nearly as crushed as I was by the experience.

Regular reality checks are important for parents who tend to get over-excited. Before putting a child forward for something at which he might fail:

- Ask an expert or the child's teacher. He will not have parental rose-tinted spectacles.
- Know your child's temperament. Will she accept endless training and advice and make the sacrifices necessary to achieve at the level required?
- Watch other children.

- Examine the odds. Your child may be the best seven-year-old tennis player in his local club, which might make him one of the top fifty seven-year-olds in this county. But there is still a long way to go before he is a national champion, let alone able to compete internationally. Can you imagine him, in a few years' time, up against those being trained up in Russia, where the programmes are intense, to become one of the top hundred players in the world.

## What help does a talented child need?

There are three stages in the development of a child's talent.

### Stage 1: The early days

Lori Ferguson of the National Association for Gifted Children finds that gifts usually become evident at an early age. Then parents can get over-excited, ploughing enormous quantities of enthusiasm into nurturing an infant talent.

In some activities it is important to start young. Ballet dancers need to develop turnout from the nursery years; likewise, the ball control needed in many sports must be established early, although the specifics of a sport can come later. Musicality, too, develops more easily if you start younger. Violinist Sarah Chang, for example, was only nine when Yehudi Menuhin described her as 'the most wonderful, the most perfect, the most ideal violinist I have ever heard'.

Tempting though it can be to develop a special talent at this young age, it is best to keep a child's interests general. Highly developed young talent attracts admiration, but there are good physiological reasons for parents not to allow a young child to pursue a passion single-mindedly. Dr Istvan Balyi, a leading expert on the development of sporting talent, thinks young children are being hot-housed for success by training pro-grammes that concentrate on an individual sport at the expense of basic training. The result will be injuries and burn-out.

He describes the problems as 'under-training and over-competing', a system created by success-driven coaches. Rather than concentrate on individual sports, he believes that between the ages of five and eight children should work to a fun-based programme based on the fundamentals of movement (running, throwing and jumping), the ABC of athleticism (agility, balance and coordination), plus speed. Children who play a variety of games develop a wider sense of what is happening, what spin is coming up on a ball, what shape the arc of the ball will take as it flies. Those who play only one sport don't have that. Another danger for children who play too intensively at a young age is that their bones can grow too fast, causing them problems with their joints.

## Stage 2: Specialising

Most coaches say that around the age of twelve is when children should stop taking on a broad range of activities or instruments and concentrate on the one at which they are most likely to excel. This can be hard for all-rounders who are good at tennis, piano, schoolwork and swimming. For girls, who are fully grown in sporting terms by the time they are sixteen, specialising at twelve leaves them four years to develop their game; boys have a further two years to go before they reach their full height and strength.

With the right attitude, it is possible for a child to start at twelve and still catch up with those who have been honing their skills from early childhood. I spoke to one coach who had reached county standard in tennis and cricket, and was also a handy footballer. He had been brought up in an unsporty family in the East End, and until the age of twelve had never done sport seriously. After he watched Wimbledon, he went to a court and found he could copy the players' actions. Shortly after, he was given a cricket trial at school and amazed the coach by being able to imitate his bowling movement perfectly.

Experts advise against too much emphasis on winning at this in-between stage. 'Some coaches teach young people in a way that doesn't allow them to develop fully,' says a tennis coach. 'At twelve they may have three good shots and may win tournaments.

But if that's how they spend their time, by the age of fifteen those three shots won't be sufficient to keep them winning. It is better to develop a broad foundation.'

As for making champions, he says: 'There are no guidelines, except discipline.'

By twelve, coaches can spot those children who have the determination to make it. 'Do they want it badly enough to come for sprints at 9 o'clock on a Sunday morning?' one athletics coach asks herself when she meets young players. At the age of twelve she had that drive, and was prepared to make any sacrifice.

**Stage 3: Crunch time**

At around the age of sixteen (girls reach their full size earlier than boys) a talented player or performer needs to decide whether the activity is going to dominate her life. By that age a player's technical level is set for life, according to Arsenal manager, Arsène Wenger. The natural capacity of one individual's muscles to contract faster than another's has been combined with good technique. What takes over then is what coaches call the 'x factor' – the competitive spirit, the will to win.

A fitness coach observes of this age group that, 'Those with the most ability have the worst work ethic. What you find is that as they get older, the hard workers overtake them, and then the talented say, "I don't want to have to start working hard because I never had to." To compete against the very best means nothing less than total commitment. It needs to be an obsession for the hard work to continue to be a pleasure.'

## What does it take to become really good?

The national performance director of British Swimming says that training for eight hours a week is sufficient for socialising, fun, participation, team-building and health, but to compete at international level it is necessary to train for 18–35 hours a week. Most clubs train for 8–14 hours a week – too much for fun, but not enough to achieve competitive results.

It takes ten years and 10,000 hours of training for athletes to achieve sporting excellence, according to Dr Istvan Balyi, adviser to Sport England. Unless they are prepared to put in the required amount of time – whether in sport, dance or music – they are doomed to be overtaken by those who are willing to give their all. And even if they are willing, they have to be prepared for disappointment due to injury: a recent survey by Ulster Coaches and Administrators said that 75 per cent of the Sports Institute squad had chronic injuries that would take some time to put right.

## Why don't children always enjoy their own talents?

A recent study of children with very high IQs found that only one out of six prodigies went on to excel, and that the rest did nothing outstanding in later life. Some may underachieve because they feel frustrated and bored. They may conceal their gifts in order to maintain friendships and gain acceptance among their peers. Some may have parents who find it hard to respond to a talented child. The same study showed that children whose exceptional abilities are not recognised and valued find life particularly hard and suffer from low self-esteem.

Noël comes from a family in which many children have shown unusual talent. Indeed, she herself was considered very gifted at art. She has known people who desperately wish to be free of their gifts, and she understands why.

'Sometimes,' she says, 'gifted children are given the impression that their gift makes them better than other people, which is a huge burden. They become uncomfortable with their gift.

'Others who are gifted with something transitory, such as beauty, can suffer terribly both when it is in full bloom and when it fades. I had one friend who felt she was losing herself as her beauty declined, who felt that anyone who didn't mention her beauty, hadn't seen her. But I had another friend who was glad when she was no longer a head-turner as it gave her the privacy to walk down a street without others saying "Wow".'

When parents tell a child how lucky he is to have a gift, that child can feel unlucky as a lot of responsibilities seem to go with it. It is a vain hope that such statements will motivate a child. 'When a child is praised for an inborn characteristic,' Noël says, 'he often feels that, since he didn't make his artistic talent or his musical gift happen, he doesn't know how to keep it happening. It is better to praise a child for something he or she can control, such as determination or a willingness to be helpful. You can't make yourself cleverer, but you can make yourself more determined or helpful.

'When I was made all too aware of my gift for art, far from building confidence, I became anxious. I felt each drawing had to be terrific, so I didn't want to draw. My art ground to a halt in my teens. I thought it wasn't enough to be quite good and enjoy doing it; I had to be very good.' Another child was always being told she was clever, and she got it into her head that scientists were clever, so she felt she had to study science even though it did not interest her.

Some parents, she finds, swamp a child with help. 'Often they rush out, get all the equipment, arrange the lessons, do all the driving and then feel let down when the child doesn't respond. The parent has taken control away from the child, so the only way the child can regain it is by being difficult.'

Another way in which parents can turn a child off a talent is by being unrealistically positive, painting a brilliant future that does not include any hard work or drudgery: 'You are so clever, you can do anything you set your mind to'. But if parents don't give the child the help and guidance he needs to achieve, the child will be stranded, unable to achieve his potential on his own.

Another relative of Noël was a harpsichordist who became, at the age of twelve, the family breadwinner. The family even moved to a different city so she could perform and earn money. She got enjoyment and recognition out of it, but she was always worried about whether she could maintain the extremely high standard required. 'The best way to nurture a talent,' Noël says, 'is to avoid letting it consume a child's whole life.'

## So how should parents help gifted children?

A top tennis coach, who was once asked to improve a girl's shots, said she couldn't as the problem was not to do with the shots, but with the girl's general confidence. 'You can only build confidence over time,' she said, 'not just by playing tennis.'

Noël agrees. She believes that parents should pay more attention to the child's temperament, habits and values than to a particular talent. Rather than focus on developing that one skill, they should foster the skills and talents needed to perform in anything – resilience, good humour, stability.

To help the child develop those desirable characteristics, parents should separate out the child from the gift and not let the child come to consider herself defined by any one talent. The child is the child and a gift is a gift.

Noël advises parents to think of a gifted child as 'just another kid who is good at something'. She is against making special provision for brilliance. One of her relatives was a composer, and the whole family tiptoed around him, whispered when he was about and were told they mustn't disturb him. 'He was given free rein to be bad-tempered and moody,' she says, 'and that's not healthy. We tend to let people who are good at things get away with murder. There is no reason why a ballet dancer can't do chores.'

But what if the ballet dancer pleads that she's exhausted? 'She may complain, but it still won't kill her. Even at the end of eight hours of practising, a quarter of an hour's washing up won't make much difference to how tired she is. She may be on her way to becoming a prima ballerina, but we don't want to train her to be a prima donna.

'We should avoid bringing people up to think they are special. So many gifted people have problems because they feel the normal rules of life don't apply to them. We shouldn't make excuses for a child and say, "Oh, he's doing that because . . ." If it is not allowed, it is not allowed.

'Gifted children are often particularly intense and can tend towards the obsessive. They may be ten-year-olds with the abilities of someone much older. Answer their questions and address their concerns according to their intellectual understanding, and also their emotional age.

'Many coaches and parents try to motivate children by telling them they can be the best. That is not useful, either on court or at home. It can breed arrogance or anxiety. Children often see through the overblown praise and soon distrust the person who is telling them they are wonderful. I suggest that parents might avoid coaches who try to motivate that way. It is quite possible to be a top athlete and a totally decent human being without arrogance. In fact, prima donnas tend not to be so successful. The way to help children to feel confident but not cocky is to stick to descriptive praise and find a coach or teacher who gives factual feedback about what a child should be doing differently, without blaming.'

What most parents want for their children is confidence. 'Confidence,' Noël says, 'is feeling that you are a worthwhile human being, regardless of whether you play tennis or not. You want a child to feel "If I never pick up a racket again, I'm still loveable – although on the court I do have a touch."'

## What about academic success?

Most parents worry constantly about academic success and exam results. Luke Scott finds this strange: 'There are very few jobs that operate like a classroom in which you have to take exams.' Writing is a bit like that, I tell him. 'Surely,' he replies, 'an ability to get on with other people and meet deadlines is more important?'

Noël agrees: 'Someone who is academically gifted may become aggressively well-read and arrogantly logical, but in most fields the ability to empathise with others is more important than the accumulation of information. Also, because very able students feel they are gifted – set apart – they can drift into poor study skills and a poor attitude to work. They then underachieve because the efficient use of intelligence depends on confidence.'

Many talented children find being put in a competitive environment at a young age saps their confidence, even if they are successful. It is distressing always to be looking upon others – and feeling looked upon – as competition. It is also very common for them to feel unconfident outside the one activity in which they shine.

'True confidence is shaped by self-reliance, by emotional security and by parents who protect a child from excessive stress,' says Noël. 'The willingness to stretch oneself calls for confidence, which comes from the development of steady, balanced relationships, not from disconnected encounters mainly with opponents.'

## How success can shape a child

Labelling a child as gifted or talented is best avoided. Professor Joan Freeman, an educational psychologist, has studied gifted children and found that those who have been labelled are much more likely to develop emotional problems than equally talented children without such a label. 'It was not the gift itself that caused the problems, but the unwelcome baggage the label brought with it,' she explains. 'Some five-year-old children are treated by their parents and schools as mini-adults, or as trophies. Some gifted children think of themselves as odd, or live in fear of not being perfect. This is bound to have repercussions.'

The daughter of a former champion tennis player has observed how that experience formed her mother's character: 'She's very black and white about everything. The ball is either in or it's out. You do or you don't win. But she is also very realistic – as she has had to be both as a player and, in later life, as a coach.'

The daughter herself had been a champion, and she found that the skills she learnt through tennis made her into an excellent executive. She found she could focus and motivate herself to win, though office life was hard to get used to after being so active. Then she dropped it all for motherhood. 'I used to have to be very disciplined,' she says, 'but now I suppose I really like being less so. Those who have had to be very self-disciplined when they are young go one way or the other: either you feel you have to keep winning, or you feel: "That's over, I'll let my hair down."'

Some might see her as having burnt out, but she considers her children to be her greatest achievement.

## Should you let a gifted child work or play above his age group?

This is a difficult question to answer. The Support Society for Children of Higher Intelligence believes it is a good thing for children who are evidently more gifted than their peers. 'Most of these children cannot relate to their age group and are academically superior. It is cruel to hold them back,' says the society's spokesperson, John Walker.

Academically, many very able children could easily cope in the year or even two years above their age, but the National Association for Gifted Children does not recommend it. Within their own age group, children who stand out often report bullying and feelings of isolation, and accelerating a child can make those problems worse. 'The risks are that emotional and social development can get left behind, storing up problems for later,' says Lori Ferguson. 'Even if there are no problems initially, when the rest of the class hits puberty the child will be much less developed and feel miserable. Or at university the child can feel left out if she is too young to go to a pub or drive a car.

'If you feel it is essential to put a child with an older class,' she says, 'talk to the child, describe what the problems might be and explore the child's feelings.'

Whether it is school or some outside activity, the same worries surface. Being viewed as a prodigy is very stressful. Looking back on the success she had before she was ten, violinist Vanessa Chang says, 'I was always the cute new face on the block. I was always longing for someone younger than me to appear so that I'd finally feel human.'

Ruth Lawrence, who, two decades ago, shot to fame at the age of twelve by going to Oxford to study mathematics – much to her father's delight – has said she will never treat her children as she was treated. In 2000 fifteen-year-old Sofia Yusof, another young prodigy, ran away from Oxford. 'Has it ever crossed your minds that the reason I left home was because I'd finally had enough of fifteen years of physical and emotional abuse?' she e-mailed her parents bitterly.

## Should I let my child try the county tennis circuit?

A mother whose teenage daughter plays well enough to go on the county tennis circuit is in two minds. 'Her chances of getting anywhere are zero,' she says, 'so should I give up my weekends to driving her around or hire someone else to?' Behind her reluctance lies a fear of the competitive instincts that top-level matches could hone. 'More than anything,' she admits, 'I am worried about the mentality. Girls are normally cooperative, but in these sports they are trained to have the killer instinct. I don't want that for her.'

One talented tennis player who reached the top fifty tells me that she is very glad she did it, even though it meant giving up school, and despite the fact that she never got further than hotels in distant places (paid for by herself) and regular disappointment. 'It gave me a sense that I can work at something and compete with the very best. I also know that, if you worry about failure, you would never attempt anything.'

## When should you let a child aim for one of the overcrowded and underpaid professions?

A mother of two singers told me that she was doing her best to steer them away from trying to make a career of it. 'Don't do it just because you are good at it,' she instructed them. 'You must do it because it is the only thing you want to do.'

Children often have an unshakeable belief in their own

destiny. For some it works: Bob Dylan was convinced he would be someone, and he is. But many find that what they need to sustain pre-eminence is not the talent that was the starting point, but all kinds of other skills, social and personal, to cope with a tough life at the top of a competitive pile. 'From the age of twelve you are going away,' says a tennis coach. 'That's hard when you are used to being ferried to and from school. That's why few girls are playing in this country.'

Allowing a child to pursue a talent will mean travel, often alone or with a chaperone. It may mean going to a special school for musicians or athletes. It will mean missing out on the friendships and sleepovers that are normal for a child of the same age. Was it good for Vanessa Mae to turn up at secondary school only once every three weeks after the age of thirteen because she was always travelling? Has Jonny Wilkinson become too isolated because he won't drink and cannot relax as all he thinks about is rugby?

Child actors often have notoriously short careers. 'As a child,' Macaulay Culkin has said, 'people just wanted me to be a kid and say things loud and open my eyes wide.' But it is not only young actors and models who have to be able to cope with perhaps finding a new career in their twenties. Many sports and artistic stars find that they cannot make a living, or don't like the way of life.

If, despite all the warnings, they still want to try, they will need to have been trained in resilience and independence.

---

**SO WHAT IS PUSHY?**

- Talking about a gift instead of a child. Sebastian Coe's father talked about 'the athlete' not 'my son'. Parents are usually less shy about admitting that a child is gifted at ballet or sport than at academic work. They should be careful about identifying the child too closely with a gift.
- Encouraging a child to show off his talents, unless specifically invited to.

- Talking constantly about the child's talent.
- Discouraging a child from trying things that he is not so gifted at in the belief that he should be concentrating on his areas of excellence.
- Demanding high performance, and punishing, sometimes with emotional withdrawal, if a child falls short.
- Finding a child acceptable when he does well, but not on any other basis.
- Expecting a child to be good at several things. Research at Columbia University found that children of twelve and thirteen from well-off families are twice as likely to suffer from depression and substance abuse as others their age because they are expected to be good at so many things.
- Forcing a child to enter competitions.
- Forgetting that the child should be doing this for himself, not for you or the club or the school.
- Making the gift into a life sentence. Don't have a narrow definition of what is worth putting your heart and soul into.

# 8

## THE LESS CONFIDENT CHILD

How do you help a child who is having difficulties at school?
Can such a child learn confidence?
How do you help a child to cope with disappointments?

In addition to addressing the problems of a child who excels, parents also need to help the child who is struggling and not doing well. Many children find some aspect of learning hard. They could feel like failures at academic work, or might be so clumsy that they consider themselves 'hopeless at games'. Some children are also socially awkward because cooperation and understanding others' perspective does not come easily to them.

Extra-curricular activities can help these children by allowing them to learn in a wider variety of ways than schools cater for. The unconfident child can learn new skills and become more generally competent. This will help his confidence and make it easier for him to do well in areas he finds difficult.

When a child is found to be dyslexic or dyspraxic, some parents use those labels as an excuse for the child not doing as well as he might. The parent who is active and positive, rather than negatively pushy, doesn't take that line. She will go through all the hoops of identifying the child's problem, then work out ways to minimise its impact on his life. This could involve seeing an educational psychologist to get a detailed assessment (and perhaps some extra time in exams). It could also mean going to a behavioural optometrist to see whether the child's eyes are working properly, or to an audiology clinic to test his hearing, or it could just mean helping with reading and organisation at home.

Whatever the diagnosis, the answer is always the same. Therapies can help, but they can't entirely remove a neurologically based obstacle to learning. Brain gym (exercises to get both sides of the brain working together) and study skills can help a child focus and organise his thoughts, and certain games can help a child become more coordinated. But these interventions are not magic wands. The child to whom something doesn't come easily will always have to work that much harder to get good results than the next child will. Left to himself, he probably won't put in the extra effort. He'll find ways to skip games or whatever activity is seen as a source of humiliation. Or he'll sit at the back of the class, giggling and becoming disruptive. And, under the bravado, he will be losing heart as he slips further behind.

This child will only keep up if the parent puts effort into making him realistic about his own shortcomings, and teaches him how to work around them. For a child who finds it difficult to learn from the written word, this could mean taping information that he has to absorb. It might mean making indexed notes on flashcards, with diagrams on one side and bullet points on the reverse. Sessions with specialist tutors (or a committed parent) can allow the child to discuss topics that would seem impossibly difficult to read about in a textbook and to acquire the component skills that others find effortless.

One of my children as he got older, found that school became more difficult. He was assessed for dyslexia, and the tests revealed his strengths and weaknesses. The results weren't surprising either to him or to anyone who knew him well, but it was reassuring to have what we already knew stated in black and white and by someone who had no previous knowledge of him. It gave us a starting point from which to work out ways in which we could help, rather than feel cornered by the problems.

As bolt-ons to school, there are many things that a positive parent can do to help a child cope better. From list-making to mind-mapping, from exercises that boost a poor short-term memory to those that improve coordination, there are numerous ways in which a parent can help a child to operate more effectively. With various of my children I have tried these strategies and found them, to greater or lesser degrees, effective.

If the problem is serious, an educational psychologist will prescribe ways to help, but parents can do a lot for a child by finding the right extra-curricular activities, then helping her become good enough at them to ensure they are a pleasure rather than a chore. A child who is wallowing in feelings of failure needs something else to think about. Luke Scott is dyslexic and did not do as well as he could have at school, but he discovered acting. 'It gave me great comfort,' he says, 'because I was also not as good at sports as some of the other boys my age.'

## How can parents help a child?

A child who has a tendency to be hyperactive, fidgety or distractible can benefit enormously from the calming effects of exercise. Noël keeps a trampoline in the corner of the classroom for children who lose concentration. Circus skills, such as juggling, are good for developing eye-hand coordination and the ability to sustain focus on a task. Activities that have many rules, such as fencing, are good for discipline.

What matters is not just the activity itself, but the approach that you and the teacher or coach take within that activity. Music, for example, can be taught in an unpressurised, exploratory way, and one board (the National College of Music) even sets exams that are less intimidating. Very dyslexic children will find it hard to learn to read music, but they could enjoy a gentler, more auditory-based alternative. As I learnt from the mother of a badly brain-damaged child, music is located in the deepest part of the brain, way below the motor and cognitive functions. As a result, many children who cannot appreciate or achieve much else can gain real pleasure from music classes.

On the other hand, another mother let her dyslexic child give up her instrument when it became too much of a struggle: 'She wasn't enjoying the practice,' she says, 'and was already overstressed coping with dyslexia at school, which meant more effort on the reading front. Learning an instrument is like learning another language, and it was just too much for her.'

It's important to choose the activity to suit the individual. A sociable child, for example, might find learning a musical instrument lonely, unless she is playing with other people, while a solitary child might find team sports confusing and upsetting. That doesn't mean the child shouldn't be helped to develop his weaker side, but requiring a child to do something that goes against the grain calls for lots of preparation and a great deal of support and encouragement in the form of descriptive praise and reflective listening at every stage.

A mother whose children are dyspraxic signed both of them up for piano tuition because it is good for coordination. 'You have to use two hands and read two lines of music; I think it helped them a lot,' she says.

Noël has reservations, however, about parents who put children in for activities that they are not good at to help them improve. 'This can lead to huge frustration. Unless the teacher or coach really knows how to teach the basic microskills that the child needs to learn, much more would be gained from signing the child up for something he is good at.'

Often parents think that art classes will be good for children who need to express themselves more fully, either because they are frustrated by a learning difficulty, or because they have had a distressing experience – family illness or divorce – for which they need an outlet. Noël recommends that, rather than put such children in an art class, parents find out about specialist 'integrative arts therapy' – though the activity does not, of course, need to be presented to the child as anything more than a fun opportunity to draw and paint.

Sometimes what begins as a remedial activity can become a full-blown passion. I recently watched a remarkable ten-year-old dance the leading role with the London Children's Ballet. That child had been taken to ballet lessons from the age of two because she was pigeon-toed; her mother thought that learning to turn her feet out would help her. She discovered a passion for it, and her ankles, legs and feet have been strengthened to such a degree that all trace of the original disability has gone. Ballet, of course, is marvellous for a child with bad posture.

A mother of a dyspraxic child was worried that he wasn't as good at anything as his elder brother. 'In class he was completely mute,' she says. 'He was not doing well at reading or writing, and his violin teacher said he would never be any good because the instrument is too technically demanding.

'I felt he was being judged according to things that he couldn't do, and I wanted to discover what he could do, so I pushed him – yes, pushed him – into singing lessons. He has blossomed, and he now has much more confidence speaking out in class because he has got used to being on a stage and performing.'

Another child in much the same position, of feeling less capable than his brother, had to be put under considerable pressure to learn tennis and sailing. Often his mother wondered if she was helping his confidence or destroying it. But by the age of twelve he has become able to hold his own on the tennis court. That was good enough for them, so they were bowled over when they went out as a family on a boat. When a gale blew up, this boy was the one who volunteered to crawl out to the stern clutching a rope to secure a sail while his elder brother sat looking terrified in the cabin.

## Tutors and private lessons

A staggering number of children have private tutoring outside school to help them keep up academically or prepare them for competitive secondary school exams. Most parents consider such private lessons to be uncontroversial. In addition to these, Noël advises parents to think about giving children private lessons in a far wider range of activities to help them keep up.

She has recommended, for example, private gym lessons for a dyspraxic child so that he could keep up with his class in PE, and private swimming lessons to help a child overcome her terror of the water so that she can join in with her group lessons. 'Few parents,' she says, 'think of doing this, but it can be just what a child needs. It is best to present the lessons as a bonus, rather than as remedial work, so the child doesn't think anything is wrong with him.'

## Teaching children to problem solve

Simple domestic tasks, such as laying the table, can be quite effective at helping children to solve certain problems. These activities teach them to observe, to perform the steps in the correct order and to realise – if we don't answer their unnecessary questions – that they know more than they think. Requiring children to help at home gives them more confidence to tackle tasks outside the home.

## Think of the upside

If a child finds just one thing at which she can shine, it is easier for her to be motivated to work hard at it and come to see it as integral to her identity. Noël warns, however, that the child who believes she has only one talent can get very wound up about it.

However mundane the talent a child discovers, Luke Scott reminds parents that it is just as worthwhile as something more prestigious – certainly in terms of learning lessons about perseverance. 'Whatever someone is learning to do, whether it is to cook a meal, help an elderly relative, or make a speech, it is a transferable skill,' he says. 'Excellence in anything teaches you attention to detail. When I was a waiter I found that the better I did the job and the more I cared about making the most of every detail of the experience, the more I enjoyed it.'

## Will becoming Scouts and Guides make children more sociable?

Many children are enrolled in Scouts and Guides, Cubs and Brownies, Noël observes, because they are initially either not very coordinated or not very sociable. The parents hope that these clubs will help them improve. Depending on the skills of whoever is leading the pack, it can be the making of the child, or it can go dreadfully wrong.

'Parents tend to believe it,' she says, 'when people such as Scoutmasters say about themselves: "I am excellent with children." They want to believe it, but it is not always true.

'I taught a child who was very upset by the way the other children were running around wildly at Cubs. This boy was hyperactive, often rebellious and not naturally as good as others of his age at sizing up a situation to see what behaviour was acceptable. So he thought the boys were misbehaving. He did not understand what the other boys understood: that this behaviour was acceptable at play-time but not during the focussed activities. But the quiet boy didn't have a good sense of appropriate behaviour, so he had to be taught the microskills of public behaviour, whereas the other children just learned by osmosis.

'Socially-based clubs can cause problems for children with poor social skills because they call for relative maturity. Unless they are supported, children who don't have those skills would do better in an activity where the emphasis lies on a technical skill, such as kicking a ball.'

## Can you help children do well at activities such as drama?

One of my daughters longs to be an actress, but last time failed the audition for the local youth theatre. I wasn't surprised: she was young for the group, and not very confident as a performer. I wanted to help her so that she would not fail next time. Yet every time I asked her what she had been doing in her drama classes, I received the usual uncommunicative response. So I asked Noël's advice. 'Ask your daughter to show you what she did,' was the response. 'Children find showing much easier than telling.'

When she showed me, I discovered that she was working on ways to convey different emotions. We were able to practise them together. I took my turn at acting, and that prompted her to come up with more suggestions on how one might display anger or happiness. She made it into the youth theatre the following year.

## Confidence-building tips

Parents always want their child to go onwards and upwards, often before they are ready. A child gains more confidence from being the top of a lower group than from being the bottom of a higher one. Tiger Woods' father, Earl, always insisted he became dominant at one level before moving him on to the next.

One mother, who had struggled for years to give her son confidence, felt that the greatest mistake a parent could make was to 'want a child to *be* something (terribly musical/frightfully sporty, etc., etc.)' to make up for academic problems. 'Aim to be positive, for the child to be a good all-rounder if possible – or at least not to hate anything.'

The mother of a dyslexic child admitted that she persuaded him to go to a tutor by buying him a beanie baby after each lesson. I would find that onerous, but she doesn't regret it, even though, now that he is going to a French class so he can keep up with the rest of his form, she is having to bribe him with slices of pizza after each session. (Being dyslexic, languages are hard for him.) She says, 'It has made him aware of the value of money, and he often talks now of how to save me some.'

## How can I help a child who feels less talented than a sibling?

In most families there is a sibling who is older and more skilled. If the child doesn't encounter that problem at home, he will at school.

Of course, if the parent goes on to a child about the brilliance of the sibling, it is hardly surprising the child will feel discouraged. The parent is too success-orientated. 'Keep pointing out to the child that there are activities she is good at, but also be honest and discuss the fact that a particular skill doesn't come easily to her. Whether she's a natural or not shouldn't be linked to whether or not she has lessons and does her practice.'

'We don't think that matters when it comes to reading,' says Noël. 'The point is to learn to do it, however long it takes. So why is it important with anything else that we think worth learning?'

## Helping over inevitable disappointments

Some disappointments are unforeseeable – injuries, illnesses, bad draws and so on. But there are some predictable disappointments that parents must prepare their children for. Every boy treble's voice will break one day, and a parent should not just make sure the child is prepared for it, but have some replacement activity ready to fill the gap.

'My son's voice broke on the afternoon before he was due to perform,' says one mother. 'We had flown all the way to Dublin for the show. It must have been awful for him to see someone else go on in his place, but I think it is even worse for the parents. The child can be excited about moving on to the next stage of growing up, but for the mother there is no such compensation; she will mourn the fact that her child is no longer a little boy.'

That child had instrumental music to throw himself into when the singing stopped, but he has kept up vocal training. 'The teacher says that a child whose voice was trained before it broke is more likely to have a good voice later,' his mother says.

Anxious parents who protect their children from disappointment are likely to make it worse for the child. When I took one of my children along to audition for *Chitty Chitty Bang Bang* – more for my benefit than hers, since she didn't seem particularly interested – I saw parents who seemed desperate for their children's success. Not only had they made sure the children knew all the words of the songs they would have to sing, they were encouraging them to sing loudly in the street.

The casting agents had said they were looking for children under a certain height, and some of the parents had put their

children in ballet shoes so that they did not exceed the requirement. When the measuring stick came round some even told
their children to crouch slightly to knock a further inch off their
height. Those children were weeded out at a later stage and were
mortified, but it was the parents who had set them up to fail.

Noël teaches a handy technique (the idea of Barbara Sher,
who wrote *Wishcraft*) for helping a child get over disappointment. 'Let's say your child wants to be an opera star, but didn't
start training soon enough, or perhaps his voice is not good
enough,' she says. 'Help him to discover the "touchstone", the
thing about singing opera that he thinks would be so wonderful.
It might be standing up in front of an audience. He can meet that
need by performing in amateur dramatics. It might be singing in
Italian. He can do that in the bath.'

## Should you tell a child that she isn't good enough?

Noël taught a girl who was ballet mad. 'She was keen to be a
dancer, did four lessons a week and was often the one who was
asked to show how good her turnout was. Soon she came to
cherish dreams of being a ballerina. However, the teachers did
not think she had a career ahead of her, and her parents wanted
to help her face that blow.'

Noël's advice was to gently but firmly help the child become
more realistic. 'The parents found a list of ballet companies, and
asked each one for information on how many of their dancers
would dance solos and how often. Then they showed their daughter
the research. Instead of telling her that she wasn't good enough, they
helped her to judge for herself. "You might be one of the lucky
ones," they said. "Do you think you are good enough to be a star?"

'The child's face showed the struggle going on in her mind:
she was having to give up a dream that had sustained her. The
parents felt cruel, as if they were ripping out her life support, and
at first she didn't want to answer. Tears came to her eyes. They
were feeling sorry for her. They were thinking of saying, "You
know, if you really try hard, you can be anything you want." But

at the end of half a minute – which is a long time for a child – the girl said, "Maybe and maybe not."

'When she said "maybe not" a cloud seemed to lift from her. There's a bereavement when a dream dies, but it is often a relief. Children need to be helped to see things as they are. They can tune out the vague advice, but they can't avoid the black and white.

'At first the parents weren't sure if they should have taken her dream away. But once the girl accepted that she wasn't going to be a star, she enjoyed the ballet lessons all the more because she didn't have to worry about getting to the top of the tree.'

## Training a child to be resilient

Disappointment is something that looks far easier to deal with than it actually is when you are encountering it. Experiencing such feelings myself at tennis lessons has made me more under-standing of my children's feelings when faced with setbacks. I have become aware of how all-consuming something that is 'only a game' can be when you are playing it: I have often felt like a ten-year-old when I have missed a shot. It is very hard indeed not to feel wretched, assume all is lost, flounce off or cry. It has also made me aware of how cheering it is when someone says something truthful but upbeat, such as, 'That serve would have been a winner if you had thrown the ball just a little higher.'

A father of a tennis player taught him to overcome disap-pointment and keep going by playing simple ball games with him. Father and son would race against each other, playing games that involved carrying balls on a racket from one basket to another. When the child dropped a ball, the father was delighted that his son kept playing, even though he was now bound to lose. 'Another child might give up and walk away after fumbling the ball. That child would turn into a quitter,' he said. He gives his son masses of descriptive praise for aspects of the game that might have seemed unimportant to the child, such as perseverance and a positive attitude, but which the father felt were the most impor-tant of all in the long run.

## Should I require my child to take part in performances?

Some children are fearful of making fools of themselves when taking part in concerts or shows. What I have found works with a stage-frightened child is to take the spotlight off her by helping her to concentrate on the event as a whole, rather than on her particular role in it. This shift in emphasis needs to take place well in advance, with chats about what form the concert will take, who will be there, whether the seats are comfortable – all the less scary aspects of it. Help the child to visualise the event, and reflectively listen to her worries.

To give the child confidence, make sure to arrive in good time, with all the right bits of kit. Make sure that she knows where you mean to sit, in case she wants to catch (or avoid) your eye. After the event, when the child has survived, forgo 'I told you so' in favour of interested comments about what was played, etc.

One mother was very nervous for her eleven-year-old son before he sang a solo flanked by real celebrities in front of a packed stadium. 'I had been at music competitions and had seen how much better girls of that age are at understanding the difference between rehearsal and performance,' she said. 'Girls seem to be better at communicating: they realise that a performance is not just about singing the notes, but about doing your very best.

'As we stood waiting to go on, my son said his legs were shaking. I said, "That's fine, you'd expect that. Let's do some deep breathing." Despite his nerves, as soon as he got on stage he was perfectly all right and came off stage delighted with himself. "I had Will Young on one side of me and Miss Dynamite on the other," he said. 'After that everything else in life will be boring.' But that's another problem.

Another mother was anxious for her daughter, who caught a cold just before her first performance in a West End musical. Instead of talking about how it might go wrong, she took the child to the park and the two of them went for a run. The mother encouraged her daughter to concentrate on the applause at the end and not to worry about the performance she had to give. Again, it was fine.

## How do you deal with a child who gets wound up because he's no good?

Noël has a story about a four-year-old whose parents came to see her. 'The child's father loved golf, and often took the boy to the driving range with him. The child had become extremely familiar with the routine and could talk a good game, but, of course, because of his age, he couldn't actually play golf. He would swing, but not actually hit anything, and he got very upset about this.

'His parents gave him a miniature set of clubs, which was the accepted thing to do, but the boy had the temperament that likes to do things well before being exposed to doing anything in public. There are some sensitive, perfectionist children who don't like to be seen learning, and those children, of course, tend to be show-offs and very sensitive.

'So when he missed the ball he used to dissolve into major tantrums, throwing his clubs around and even hitting his dad. His father, a mild-mannered man, was mystified, and wondered if he should stop taking the boy to the golf course, even though they had a lovely time seeing friends and having lunch in the clubhouse.

'Of course, it wasn't in this area alone that the boy had unrealistically high expectations of himself. His mother noticed it in other ways too, but this was the area where his dad noticed it. The father considered switching his visits to the golf course to a different day so he could go without his son. He even stopped talking about golf at home because the boy had started saying that he hated golf.

'I advised that he should do exactly the opposite. He should keep taking the boy to the driving range and keep talking about golf with him. What he oughtn't to do was reassure him – "You'll be good at it one day" or "It's just because of your age that you can't hit the ball." Reassurance is rarely reassuring. At first the parents thought my advice was cruel. What they hadn't realised was that the golf wasn't the real problem. The real problem was that the parents were hostages to the boy's moods. He was highly strung, and the parents had actually been fearing his tantrums. Their reactions had not only made him more upset about golf, but were also threatening to ruin his relationship with his father.

'Parents are often tempted to tiptoe around a sensitive child's upset. They try to avoid mentioning the problem. I say that parents should do the opposite: keep mentioning it. At first your child will complain or throw a tantrum each time he hears that he will have to do what he doesn't want to do, but if you carry on saying, "On Saturday we are having lunch with X at the golf course" or "Let's go to a film after we've played golf . . .", the child will get used to the dreaded activity and he will forget to make a scene.

'Very soon, when the boy saw that his tantrums didn't get him attention, he stopped behaving so badly. He still kept trying at golf and, interestingly but not surprisingly, when he had a better attitude and didn't throw tantrums, he did get better and was actually quite good.'

---

**WHAT'S PUSHY?**
- Finishing tasks for a child because he is too slow.
- Managing children's time very closely, making 'to do' lists for them.
- Hovering over children while they do things, implying that they need lots of help or correction.
- Getting physically involved in homework, rubbing out mistakes, colouring in, redrawing lines.
- Pointing out mistakes immediately, instead of letting a child notice an error in his own time.
- Setting a new goal as soon as the current one has been reached.
- Seeing carelessness as a sign of future failure.

# 9

# BEHAVIOUR AND THE BUSY CHILD

Do busy children have to behave badly?
When to use an activity to make a child behave better at home.
How to prevent sibling rivalry.

How a child spends her time, and who she spends it with, will inevitably shape her personality. That is why parents are so keen to get children off the sofa and out playing sports or developing artistic interests. Left to their own devices, slumped in front of the television or het up by the constant stimulus of a computer game, a child will not only be less fit and accomplished than one who has a wide range of active interests, she will also have acquired bad psychological habits of passivity and isolation.

But however beneficial many extra-curricular activities can be, they can also become an excuse for bad behaviour, unless a parent is aware of the dangers. I am constantly faced with children who claim to be too tired to help around the house after three hours' gym, or too nervous to be good tempered because they have a show coming up. My children use my insistence on practising to argue and complain. They also fight with each other over who is allowed to do what activity.

This drives me mad because when a child has chosen to do something and I am paying for it, I want the results (unreasonably, I know) to be 100 per cent positive. I feel the child should not only be learning whatever skill it is, but also strength of character. I feel the child should be becoming more mature, not using their activities as excuses to be babyish.

When an activity becomes a stick to beat me with, I worry that the child is doing too much, or that the activity is too competitive and stressful. I don't for a minute imagine any of my children winning Wimbledon at the age of seventeen, like Boris Becker, but I do fear them feeling and behaving as he did under the pressure to succeed. As a teenager, Becker so defined himself by his tennis that when he lost he would be incredulous and, like a petulant child, would throw tantrums. To cope, he would shut himself in his car, 'listen to music and scream and yell and cry unseen'.

Cries of 'I'm bored' are also guaranteed to wind me up. No one wants their children to lack self-motivation, and that is a particularly painful prospect for those of us who fear we may have given our children too many opportunities. The hot-housed child is generally considered to be lacking in inner resources because he has never had to make a choice and stick to it; someone else – the parent or the coach – has always done that for him. In later life there won't be a parent around to answer the question 'What are we doing now?'

Like most parents, what I want is for my children to become more pleasant and cooperative, not less so, as a result of all the team and individual activities they do. I want them to feel confident and fulfilled, but not at the expense of others in the family. What I want, of course, is not something that these activities in themselves can supply – though the habits of mind they inculcate may help or hinder the process.

Teachers and coaches have expert knowledge, and can be more or less skilled at handling groups of children, but training a child to behave well is homework for the parent. Training is not the same as teaching. Training is getting a child to repeat desired behaviour so often that it becomes a habit.

As I learnt when I took parenting classes from Noël and Luke (see *How to Be a Better Parent*), the prerequisite for children who are a pleasure to be with is a parent who is positive, firm and consistent, who has thought about what matters and what doesn't, who sets boundaries, rewards good behaviour, doesn't allow the child to get away with misbehaviour, and teaches a child to think and act for himself. Although I had already learnt the sixteen skills that Noël recommends to parents who want to get better at the job of child-training, I still found myself flummoxed by some behavioural questions.

## Why do children behave less well in extra-curricular activities than they do at school or at home?

Many generally well-behaved children can become unruly when they go to clubs after school and at weekends. I've witnessed some wild scenes at Cubs, with the pack leaders seeming unable to marshal the screaming hordes, and have even been asked politely to remove children from weekend art classes because of disruptive behaviour.

Noël believes the problem arises because school is structured, while extra-curricular activities tend to be less rigid in format. Structure often boils down to clear expectations: rules, routines, rewards and consequences. When there is insufficient structure, most children will soon drift into behaving in ways that they would never dream of in a more structured setting. 'Sometimes,' she says, 'behaviour problems can arise because the extra lessons involve energetic movement, which can lead to chaos if not contained. In other cases it is because creative activities are often taught by artistic types, free spirits, who don't think in terms of structure.

Also, many teachers and coaches suffer from the worry that if the activity isn't fun for the children all the time, they won't want to come back. The coach may not know how to help children accept that there are dull bits in every activity.'

### Using extra-curricular activities as a reward

When a child is obsessed by wanting to do something, it can mean he is tempted to pay scant attention to other, less exciting areas of his life. Rather than allow this to happen, a parent can use the child's motivation to influence him to behave in ways that the parent considers desirable and important. Because parents give too much too easily, children come to expect as their birth-right all these expensive activities and equipment and all the parental ferrying. Rather than letting children take all this for granted, parents can teach children about earning. Extra-curricular activities can be used as leverage to make that point.

When she was in her early teens actress Keira Knightley used to badger her parents to get her an agent. They could see she wasn't going to give up, but they made it a condition of getting her an agent that she had not only to do her schoolwork every day during the holidays, but smile about it too. Similarly, golfer Justin Rose's mother allowed him to turn professional only on condition that he read the newspaper every day; she didn't want him to be as narrowly focused as tennis champion Monica Seles, who, when invited to see Notre Dame in Paris, asked if it was a band or a football team.

Noël had a pupil, a teenage girl, who used to dress up like a mini Britney Spears, wearing tiny skirts and exposing acres of tummy, which worried her mother. 'The girl was very keen on riding. When she rode she had to wear the right uniform and, to her mother's surprise, she made no fuss about it. But the mother was still very worried about getting her daughter to dress properly for going to a wedding or visiting her grandparents. It soon came out that dressing inappropriately was not the only problem. The girl was bunking off school and not doing her homework. The mother was intimidated by the child's sarcastic manner and felt powerless.

'I suggested that the mother use the riding as a reward, not as a right. Obviously this wouldn't work if the activity were one you were trying to entice a child into. First, the riding became contingent on her going to school, doing her work and being polite. Initially the reward had nothing to do with how she dressed; that came a bit later. At first the girl was furious, as she had never before had to earn the right to take part in expensive gymkhanas every fortnight.

This mother was worried that the switch to earning would alienate her daughter. The girl did complain initially that her mother was trying to ruin her life! I advised the mother to do lots of descriptive praise and reflective listening, to make it easy for the daughter to earn the activity she loved and to keep demonstrating that she believed the girl would earn the riding. So she kept saying things such as, "You are on track for earning your riding this week", or "You are doing everything necessary to earn your riding". The girl couldn't be upset for long as the mother was so positive.

'The mother soon saw that earning the activity worked, partly because the daughter needed to be driven to the stables. I had told the mother that she had to earn the lift by helping around the house and dressing sensibly. On a few occasions she didn't earn the lift and couldn't go.

'As soon as she saw how her choice of clothing impacted on her activities, she toned down her dress considerably. She said she had got bored of looking like that, but the change was too quick for that to be the reason. I think she no longer felt she had to be the very opposite of her family. She became a valued member of her family and of her school.'

Noël has another story of how parents used a much-loved activity as a means to getting children to do their best in other areas. In this case, the two boys in a family were both excellent sailors, but they were not doing their work at school. 'I recommended to the parents that the children should have to bring home a "B" or better in every subject each week in order to earn their boating at the weekend. The parents were originally quite wimpish: they said the kids would be so angry that they would stop working altogether, but in fact it was very effective. The programme soon became known in the family as "B for Boat".

'The parents did not want to create any additional work or hassle for the teacher. So they typed up and photocopied a form that simply had to be signed by each teacher each Friday. On a couple of occasions the boys blew it because the form wasn't entirely filled in. They said they had had supply teachers on the Friday, but that wasn't a good enough excuse: a supply teacher could still say whether the work had been of "B" standard that day.

'Those boys went from being very spoilt kids, who allowed all criticism to just roll off their backs, to "B" students, who started to enjoy school as, of course, they were bound to when they started putting some effort into it. Initially, they were outraged that they had to curtail some midweek activities in order to do the homework and revision that would earn them their time on the boat. Soon they stopped complaining.'

Once again, she says, there was a happy ending – as there almost always will be so long as parents are prepared to act on the advice they came looking for.

## Letting a child have limited choices

Sometimes, when a child is behaving badly, it is a way of signalling that she needs to have more control over her own life. My twelve-year-old made my life a misery complaining about studying both the oboe and the piano. She had chosen to do both, but that didn't prevent her treating me like a monster for insisting she stick to her decision. Eventually I weakened and said that she had to keep going with both for another term, since the tuition fees were paid in advance, but after that she could decide for herself about dropping one of them. Having been given the choice she decided to keep both on, and since then has spent much less time grumbling about practising.

---

**HOW CAN YOU TELL IF YOUR CHILD IS NOT FEELING PUSHED?**

A parent will know that the child does not feel under pressure by the following signs:

- Enjoyment of the activity
- Accepting challenges, rather than complaining
- Gradual improvement
- Looking forward to the activity (most of the time)
- Making friends
- Learning, developing and understanding new concepts (children themselves won't notice they are developing; they just think they are the way they are)
- Blossoming self-confidence

---

## How children signal too much pressure

Many activities are very intense – as are the children who do them. The young chess player Magnus Carlsen sometimes forgets to eat because he gets so engrossed in a game that can last for five or six hours. Chess is something that can reduce adults to tears and tantrums, so parents have to be watchful for the signs that a child is overstressed.

Often children don't want to say they are nervous, or that something is too difficult for them. But the tension has to come out somewhere, so they misbehave. A child who feels she is going to lose a match might go to the loo constantly during the game, destroying her own and the opponent's concentration. Or she might play unbearably slowly, or keep challenging the rules, or wander off when she thinks she is about to fail.

A child may feel he has been forced to play only to make up the numbers. He is worried that he will lose as he doesn't understand the rules and assumes that the other players are brilliant so he may wreck the game by making deliberate mistakes. It is easier to get the failing over and done with than to worry.

Parents who bully, bribe and cajole will find that their children demonstrate their independence by skimping on practice and skipping lessons. The result is not just a waste of time and money, but the child can end up feeling a failure.

Signs of stress include:

- Problems sleeping
- A change in eating patterns
- Tiredness or lethargy
- Tears
- Rudeness and irritability
- Social withdrawal

Often the most harmful side of some activities is the attention that comes with doing well. What starts as an interview for a local paper can get out of hand if a child has done something extraordinary. Even a watchful parent can find it hard to draw the line, and a little attention develops into a rash of publicity and TV appearances. Then the child suffers from the hazards of being picked out in the street and lionised for being famous. He may be unable to lead a normal life.

Luke Scott knows gifted people who have chosen to keep their talent as a hobby because, if it were their work, it would be too stressful. 'I have a friend who is a rock musician, who is happy to play the local circuit,' he says. 'He is good enough to do it professionally, but he says that would take the fun out of it.'

## Why some children become isolated

Children who are very wrapped up in an external activity often don't have many friends at school. Boys who are keen on ballet are often teased. Victoria Beckham, before she became a Spice Girl, was so intent on her future career in singing and dancing that she didn't make many friends at school. Children who are very dedicated to something, or whose parents appear to offer them boundless support and encouragement, are often the object of envy.

Musical children are sometimes teased, which is why it is often reassuring for them to be in a choir and have the support of others. Of course, it doesn't help – as one boy singer said – if you are also small and plump.

Sometimes it is their own fault because they brag, but often it is simply because classmates assume they are snobbish or different – especially those children who do modelling and earn considerable sums of money, a portion of which is usually spent on their own clothes and toys. They may be out of touch with what others are talking about because they are so wrapped up in their own activity.

Some children have the confidence just to go out and be normal. Chess champion Magnus Carlsen knew that everyone at his new school was expecting him to be a nerd, but when he turned up he showed them that he wasn't. Too often, though, protective parents make the problem worse by sympathising too much with a child, encouraging the feeling of being special instead of assuming that a certain amount of teasing is normal for any child and telling the child to get on with it.

It often shocks naturally gifted players when someone who isn't as good, but is more friendly and helpful, gets chosen for a team in their stead. 'The child can be mystified,' says Noël, 'that no one wants to play with him. "I'm better, why don't they want me?" the child thinks.'

Often a parent can see exactly why, but it is not so easy to get the point across. 'When parents explain it falls on deaf ears,' she finds. 'It is better, when a child complains, for the parent to ask how come it happened. The child may say, "Because they don't like me". Don't at that point reassure the child that of course he is well-liked. Instead, ask further questions. "What is it about you, do you think, that they may not like?" This helps to make the child more self-aware. The least effective way to teach is to tell or lecture. When a child has to think about the effect he has on others, he is more likely to change.'

If a child is behaving in a starry way, sometimes actually doing the activity professionally instead of fantasising about it can make him more down to earth. One girl who had a major part in a theatrical show emerged nicer after three months (it was other parents who said this, not her own) and more popular for it, as she had seen how small and unimportant she was in the context of the production. At her drama class she was used to being the star.

## What do I do about the child who is a bore?

This child has restricted or narrow interests, and bores and irritates other children by talking of little apart from his pet subject. Noël's advice is that the parents should insist that the child regularly talks about other things. 'Often,' she finds, 'the child isn't clear about what he is required to do. Perhaps he has heard the parents disagreeing on the matter. Or the parents may have shown that they were not in charge by giving in, or by pleading and lecturing.'

This hyperfocus on one activity can occur when a child thinks he is only good at that one thing. With our guitar-mad child, we had a crisis on holiday when he burnt his finger snuffing out a candle. Because he could no longer play his guitar, he felt he had lost his role in the group of teenagers. After a day of deep depression, he emerged from his room, joined in with other activities, and gained enormous confidence from realising he wasn't just a guitar player.

## What do I do about a child who is more comfortable with adults than with his contemporaries?

Many only children feel more comfortable with adults than with their own age group, and so do children whose extra-curricular activities bring them into an adult world. Actress Jane Asher says: 'I got offered my first film, *Mandy*, and then I became addicted. It wasn't the fame. It was more being with grown-ups, being treated in an exciting way, being on the set, having food brought to you, not being at school. And pretending to be someone else. After that I can't remember ever thinking that this wouldn't be what I'd do.'

She was fortunate in that she managed to carry on with her acting career. Many don't. 'If they have done a lot of professional acting as children, they rarely want to carry on,' says Stephanie Manuel, founder of Stagecoach, which has nearly 300 branches all over the country. 'They'll be sickened by it. What little magic there is in performing will go.'

When children spend their time with adults or on adult projects they can be considered precocious or 'stuck-up' by their own age group. To avoid this, a parent can insist on a child taking up other activities that involve team games with contemporaries. If the child does seem to be developing an unfortunate manner, it's worth asking him to reflect on why others react badly to him. Of course, the parent also has the option of keeping the child away from acting or modelling for a while.

Many young actors do stop for a while. After appearing in *The Parent Trap*, Lindsay Lohan took several years out to be a normal child at high school, and it didn't make it harder for her to land the leading role in *Mean Girls*. If anything, knowing how ordinary children behave made her better able to interpret the role of the outsider who so wants to be popular that she behaves as badly as the worst of her contemporaries.

## What do you do when a child wants to dominate?

I spoke to one woman who was embarrassed that her daughter, who longs to perform, is always insisting on doing shows when her friends come round. The child bosses the proceedings, takes the main parts and best costumes, puts other children down and throws tantrums if thwarted. 'I try to explain to her what other children are thinking, but I don't want to hurt my daughter's feelings by being too critical,' says her mother.

Rather than protect the child's feelings, the mother should prepare for success by having numerous talk-throughs with the child, before the playdates, about how other children might feel and what behaviour is required of her. Descriptively praise all attempts at sharing the limelight.

## How to deal with a child who feels in charge

When children do well and the parent spends a lot of time serving their interests – even managing the money they earn – it can cause problems. Roles become blurred. Children can see themselves as the one in charge because they have a career that may be more financially successful than the parent's. Very clever children can often argue in a rational way – even when they are being irrational – and challenge a parent's authority, as well as trying his patience.

But a successful child isn't always a recipe for disaster. I was very impressed when I met Haley Joel Osment, the star of *The Sixth Sense*, and his father (a less successful actor). The child had a most respectful attitude to his father, a serious but not starry-eyed attitude to his own work, and perfect manners.

Parents are almost always their child's manager at the

beginning of a career. Long term there are often problems when a parent controls the purse-strings, arranges a timetable, and accepts or declines work, but short term the parent is more likely than anyone else is to protect the child's interests. For the relationship to work it needs to be clear who is in charge. The child can decide if he will take a part or enter a tournament. The parent decides on bedtime.

There will always come a sticky point when the child becomes old enough to take charge of her own affairs. Depending on how positive or negative the parent has been and how well he or she has prepared the child for independence, the shift can go well or badly. Singer Charlotte Church is still close to her mother/ex-manager, but violinist Vanessa Mae won't see hers; only through a complete rift can she make the point about now being in charge of her own life.

*Home Alone* star Macaulay Culkin had a father who managed him aggressively. So demanding and manipulative was Culkin Senior that many producers refused to consider the boy for roles. Eventually, not only his wife, but also his son, divorced him.

It is possible that better handling of the situation earlier on might have avoided the break. 'A family came to see me,' says Noël, 'whose daughter had been making money from commercials. She was given as pocket money only a small fraction of what she earned; most of the money went into a trust fund, and the parents spent a little of it on getting a better car and having a family holiday. Nevertheless, the girl thought of herself as very special because other kids weren't earning money, and also because her parents deferred to her so much. She felt she had a hold over them. Unintentionally, they had created a little monster. For the camera she could assume an air of adorable innocence, but offstage she was a horrible little girl, and the parents came to me because of her bad behaviour.

'I said, "She needs to earn her spending money by following the family rules and doing some household chores every day. And she's not to have any more of a say in things than her siblings do just because her money has contributed to them happening." Also, instead of it always being the mother who took the girl to auditions, I asked the father to accompany her as often as he could because the mother had become practically her servant and dresser.

'Before long, the girl became a regular member of the family again. She learnt that what she was contributing was no more special than what her siblings were doing.'

## How to prevent sibling rivalry

When one child has a talent that he wants to pursue whole-heartedly it can be very time-consuming, and the rest of the family can feel left out and resentful. Noël's advice to parents is to take just as much interest in the siblings' activities as in those of the especially talented child.

Sometimes siblings want to be involved, particularly if a brother or sister's talent is taking them to interesting places. Teenage golfer Justin Rose used to ask his brother to caddy for him. It wasn't always a success, he admits. 'I was so uptight that if he hadn't cleaned my ball and handed it back to me within five seconds, I would shout at him. It was ridiculous.' Several years on, however, they can laugh about it, and the brother is glad to have been involved.

Often the problem with a child who is pursuing an activity doggedly is that one parent is always the one involved. It frequently seems to work out that fathers are the chief support if an activity involves lots of driving and time away from the home, but it is also common for mothers and sons to team up, or fathers and daughters. This can create jealousy. Noël suggests that parents split up the ferrying and sitting around on the sidelines so it is not a one-parent one-child team. 'If one parent is more available, it may be easier for that one to do the ferrying,' she acknowledges, 'but then the other one can do it at half-term or at weekends.

'Sometimes the problem is not so much the amount of time

the parent spends with a child as that the child's special talents or opportunities are talked about so much. Each child's triumph should be given exactly the same treatment and the same "air time". Regardless of how talented or driven one child may be, parents should put the same enthusiasm and the same time into the others.'

The father of one young girl who excels at tennis told me that he makes a point of playing ball games with both his children, and keeps them fun and easy so that the other child does not feel inferior. Aware of the other child's feelings, he never discusses tennis in front of that child, and at mealtimes conversation is kept general.

A mother whose daughter does athletics at an international level says that she showed talent at a very early age. Suspecting that this might cause problems with the other children, the mother made extra efforts to bring all her children up to be very independent. The daughter was made to take herself by bicycle to the track from an early age so that the mother did not have devote so much time to ferrying her around. When the mother did have to travel to a competition with her daughter, the other children were used to looking after themselves, so they didn't miss the mother's presence nearly as much as they might have done if they had been used to her doing everything for them.

## How do you deal with siblings who want to exclude one another?

In my family we have several times had tearful scenes because a child wants to participate in an activity that one of her siblings is already doing. The friction occurs particularly between the three girls, who are close together in age. Each likes to establish some territory among activities that she considers inviolably hers and guards this jealously. When a younger sister wanted to take up the same activity there were terrible tantrums, despite large amounts of descriptive praise and reflective listening.

Eventually, we found ways round these problems. The child who had been prevented from doing gymnastics by her elder sister tried athletics instead (she strained an ankle on day one, but is still keen to do more); and the one who wanted to take up the violin, but couldn't because that was already bagged, is starting the viola.

## What about siblings who won't take an interest?

I spoke to one rather sad teenage athlete whose school friends were proud of her achievements, and often came to watch and cheer her on in competitions, but whose brother and sister 'refused' to come. No doubt the siblings were fed up with the father making their sister the centre of the universe. What would Noël do? Even though this situation had existed for several years, she said, it was not too late to change the atmosphere in that family for the better. 'That family is no longer pulling together as a team. The parents need to focus just as much attention on their non-star children as on the star. They should require the siblings to come along regularly to their sister's sports events, and also require her to attend her siblings' special events,' she said. 'When parents allow their children to refuse, the parents have abdicated responsibility.'

---

**WHAT'S PUSHY?**
- Losing track of the child, who is longing for attention, underneath the talent, which is getting too much attention.
- Allowing a child to use an activity as an excuse for bad behaviour.
- Focusing on a child's success to the exclusion of the rest of the family's needs.
- Getting too reliant on a child's earnings.
- Expecting a child to be an adult just because she sometimes moves in adult circles.
- Not letting a child become independent.

# CONCLUSION

Watching my children become involved in all kinds of activities, most of them ones I had never known about before, has been one of the greatest pleasures of being a parent. I don't mind too much about whether they are any good at them – though I would like them to acquire a basic competence – the point is to try things, stick with them for long enough to find out whether you like them, and then either carry on or move on.

Through taking my children about, I have had the excitement of watching performances by those who really are good. I often have to take a hanky to the ice rink on Sunday mornings because some of the children are so graceful that they move me to tears. Concerts, even at a humble level, are always affecting because of the solemnity of the efforts. So are the shows that children have rehearsed for weeks, mastering their lines and moves, regardless of the inevitable comic mishaps.

Taking the children to their lessons has brought me into contact with the unfamiliar worlds of chess and swimming, football and gymnastics. I have met teachers and coaches who have often been stars in their youth, but are now gaining as much, if not more, satisfaction from passing on their love of an activity to a younger generation. For the first time in my life I have read the sports pages of newspapers. Watching the pleasure my children have taken in acquiring new skills has got me playing tennis and swimming again. Who knows what I might try next: the piano?

At times I have worried about overstepping that invisible line into pushy parenthood. In helping children to become successful adults, it is easy to overlook the importance of raising a happy child. I know exactly when those moments occurred: when I have been too critical, rushed, unrealistic or ambitious. The conversations that have led to this book have made me far more aware of these signs and have shown me the best ways to step back over the line again into being positive and supportive.

In the end what is important – as I sometimes have to remind myself when a child is reluctant to practise – is not whether a child masters a particular level, but whether she feels successful and understands the discipline, commitment and sacrifices involved. Few of us are capable of winning an Olympic gold medal, and the despair on Paula Radcliffe's face as she abandoned her attempt at the 2004 marathon was enough to make me glad to live by smaller triumphs, lesser hurdles, to feel pleased with myself just for getting the children off to school in a calm frame of mind.

The point of all these activities is, at bottom, to learn that the way not to feel bored and isolated is to be a participant. It may be that the passion you discover in a child is one that carries through into adult life, that the football a ten-year-old plays becomes the perfect antidote to office life in his middle age. But different passions reveal themselves at different stages. In your twenties it could be travel and work. In your thirties it could be home and family. In your forties it could be helping a charity. The only habit it is important to acquire young is that of daring to get involved so that you don't have to live with the regrets for what might have been.

All of us are good at something, but unless we find out what is available we might never discover what that is.

# ACTIVITIES INFORMATION

Here is a selection of activities that you or your children might want to get involved in. Each entry offers some guidance about the pros and cons, the recommended age to start and, where possible, the approximate cost. In each case I've also noted the organisations and publications that I have found useful during my research.

## ACADEMICALLY GIFTED (COURSES FOR)

*Pros:* Extra support and courses can extend bored, bright children.
*Cons:* Being singled out as gifted can cause teasing and self-consciousness.
*Age:* Organisations help gifted children of all ages though NAGTY's courses (see below) are for 11–19-year-olds.
*Cost:* The government is pouring money into this field to stretch the most able, but private extension activities, such as those organised by Gabbitas Thring, are available; costs vary.
**Children of High Intelligence** – support group for the top 2% (5% with under 7s). Runs Saturday classes in London and Derby. Tel: 020 8347 8927. www.chi-charity.org.uk
**Gabbitas Educational Consultants** – Tomorrow's Achievers workshops. Tel: 020 7734 0161. www.gabbitas.co.uk and www.masterclasses.co.uk
**Gifted Children's Information Centre** – free counselling service and counselling support network with relation to dyslexia

and other sometimes related problems. Tel: 0121 705 4547. www.ukindex.info/giftedchildren

**National Academy for Gifted and Talented Youth** – based at Warwick, but involving universities from Exeter to Durham, this organisation offers 900 summer school places to 'enrich, not accelerate' gifted and talented children in state schools. Tel: 0247 6574212. www.warwick.ac.uk/gifted

**National Association for Gifted Children** – for those who prove, usually through tests taken at school, that they fall into the top 5 per cent of the national ability range. Advice and support for parents; local clubs for children. Tel: 08707 703217. www.nagcbritain.org.uk

**Xcalibre** – portal for the academically gifted. www.xcalibre.ac.uk

## ACTING

*Pros:* Good for general confidence and self-presentation; develops stamina and self-discipline. Post-GCSE students at stage schools leave with a teaching qualification.

*Cons:* Can lead children into careers that they cannot sustain. (For every Daniel Radcliffe amassing millions from Harry Potter, thousands earn £30 a day as extras.) Time-consuming for parents taking children to auditions, and ferrying them to and from performances.

*Age:* Classes available for four-year-olds, but most youth theatres are looking at children of eight upwards.

*Cost:* Drama courses vary widely in cost. Stagecoach, a nationwide franchise of dance/drama/singing classes, currently charges nearly £300 a term. Stage schools also charge fees, though some offer scholarships. After A-levels children can study for BTEC Higher National Diplomas in performing arts, the equivalent of A-levels. No grants available for drama schools.

**Conference of Drama Schools** – copies of their booklet are available from French's Theatre Bookshop. Tel: 020 7255 4300. www.drama.ac.uk

*Contacts* – a handbook containing comprehensive listings,

published by *Spotlight*. Available from local libraries, or tel: 020 7437 7631.

**Local theatres** – often run workshops.

**National Association of Youth Theatres** – Tel: 01325 363330. www.nayt.org.uk

**National Council for Drama Training** – Tel: 020 7387 3650. www.ncdt.co.uk

**National Operatic & Dramatic Association** – Tel: 0870 770 2480. www.noda.co.uk

**National Youth Music Theatre Festival** – Tel: 020 7734 7478. www.nymt.org.uk

**National Youth Theatre** – Tel: 01325 363330. www.nyt.org.uk

*The Stage* – weekly newspaper, essential reading for listings of auditions. www.thestage.co.uk

**Stagecoach** – Tel: 01932 254333. www.stagecoach.co.uk

## ARCHERY

*Pros:* One of Britain's surprising sporting hotspots, with medal wins in the last four Olympic Games. Equipment easy to store; lots of competitions; practised indoors and outdoors.

*Cons:* Not much exercise.

*Age:* From seven upwards.

*Cost:* £15–£20 for an introductory course of six lessons, including the use of basic equipment (bow, arrows, arm guard, finger-tab, quiver, etc). Kit costs about £100–£150 to buy. Adult club fees £350 a year; juniors less.

**Grand National Archery Society** – Tel: 01952 677888. www.gnas.org

## ART

*Pros:* Easy for parents to do with children; minimal ferrying; excellent visual training; useful and enjoyable any time, anywhere.

*Cons:* Some children are discouraged by teachers who don't allow them to learn by copying. With very young children mess can be a problem.

*Age:* Any.

*Cost:* Very low. Most galleries offer free weekend activity trolleys. A box of watercolours costs about £24.

**National Association of Decorative and Fine Arts Societies** – provides listings of local groups; offers financial awards for gifted young members; excellent holiday courses. Tel: 020 7430 0730. www.nadfas.org.uk

**Potfest** – information on classes and courses www.potfest.co.uk

## ATHLETICS

*Pros:* Excellent for general fitness and strong bones; plenty of tracks all over the country.

*Cons:* Injuries; driving to competitions; drug issues at higher levels.

*Age:* From eight upwards.

*Cost:* Little equipment needed, except for trainers. Expensive travelling to competitions, although some counties give grants.

**Amateur Athletic Association of England** – Tel: 0161 406 6320. www.british-athletics.co.uk

**National Young Athletics League** – Tel: 0161 485 8532. www.natyal.co.uk

**UK Athletics** – Tel: 0870 998 6800. www.ukathletics.net

## BADMINTON

*Pros:* All year round sport

*Cons:* Not so many play.

*Age:* From seven upwards.

*Cost:* Moderate.

**Badminton Association of England** – Tel: 01908 268400. www.baofe.co.uk

## BALLET

*Pros:* Good for posture; classes readily available all over the country; forces girls to wear their hair scraped back off their faces.

*Cons:* Can lead to strange way of standing and walking with feet turned out; boys may be teased; technique rigid.

*Age:* From two.

*Cost:* Reasonable initially. Most schools cost £100 a term for a lesson a week. Shoes, leotards, etc. not too much. At higher grades (5 and above) gets expensive, as two or more classes a week are necessary.

**Chance to Dance** – a Royal Opera House-based scheme to find London-wide dancers. Tel: 020 7212 9410. www.royalopera.org. Similar schemes are run by Birmingham Royal Ballet (Dance Track), tel: 0121 245 3500 (www.brb.org.uk), and Leicestershire Arts in Education (Dance Activate), tel: 0116 270 0850 www.leics.gov.uk

**English National Ballet** – has Youth Group for 11–15 year-olds, who may not have dance experience. Tel: 020 7581 1245. www.ballet.org.uk

**London Children's Ballet** – produces an annual highly professional show. Tel: 020 8969 1555. www.londonchildrensballet.com

**Northern Ballet** – Youth dance groups for children aged eight upwards. Tel: 0113 2745355. www.Northernballettheatre.co.uk

**Regional listings** of local dance and other arts groups – www.ukchildrensdirectory.com

## BASKETBALL

*Pros:* High action sport; good for scholarships to US colleges.
*Cons:* Finding courts; height helps.
*Age:* From seven upwards.
*Cost:* Very low.

**England Basketball** – Tel: 0870 7744225. www.england basketball.co.uk

## BOXING

*Pros:* Street cred; good for letting off steam.
*Cons:* Broken noses; some see it as institutionalised violence.
*Age:* From nine; competitions from 11.
*Cost:* Low. Junior affiliation £6 per year; classes around £2.

**Amateur Boxing Association of England** – Tel: 020 8778 0251. www.abae.co.uk

## BROWNIES & GUIDES

*Pros:* Social; lots of different craft activities; lots of outings.
*Cons:* Slightly uncool image.
*Age:* From six upwards.
*Cost:* Low monthly membership fee.
**Girlguiding UK** – Tel: 020 7834 6242. www.girlguiding.org.uk

## CANOEING

*Pros:* Good for general fitness and mental alertness; shy kids learn
to cooperate with others in boats; fun to race; can make swift
progress.
*Cons:* Less socially useful than sailing.
*Age:* From eight, when children have sufficient strength and can
swim.
*Cost:* Low.
**British Canoe Union** – Young People's Programme has developed
a number of initiatives: the Paddlepower Scheme, Cadet
Leader Award, Top Club, Diamond Slalom Award. Tel: 0115
9821100. www.bcu.org.uk

## CARDS

*Pros:* Good for social life, holidays and mental arithmetic.
*Cons:* No exercise; can become compulsive and lead to gambling.
*Age:* Never too young for 'Pairs'.
*Cost:* Minimal, until they get into poker.
**American Contract Bridge League** – website has some good free
software. www.acbl.org
**English Bridge Union** – offers a simplified version (mini-bridge)
to introduce children to the game. Cheap weekend of junior
tuition in September at Loughborough before term starts.
Tel: 01926 317200. www.ebu.co.uk
**Local bridge clubs** – details available from libraries.

## CHESS

*Pros:* Good for thinking under pressure, both tactically (next few
moves) and strategically (game plan); also good for the

memory. Character building: you have to imagine what your opponent is up to.

*Cons:* Nerdy image; very competitive; not many girls play, but that's changing.

*Age:* From three or four. Hard at first, so start with fewer pieces.

*Cost:* Low. Millfield School in Somerset offers a Nigel Short Chess Scholarship for 7–16 year-olds.

**British Chess Federation** – Tel: 01424 775222. www.bcf.org.uk

## CIRCUS ARTS

*Pros:* Good for balance, concentration and coordination; opportunities for disabled participation.

*Cons:* Not many places offer courses.

*Age:* From any age depending on the activity.

*Cost:* From £1–10 per session, depending on group; £25 for a day course.

**National Association of Youth Circus** – umbrella organisation for youth groups. Tel: 01706 650676. NAYC@skylight-circus-arts.org.uk

**Skylight Circus Arts** – trains children of all ages. It also represents the NAYC (above). Tel: 01706 650676. www.skylight-circus-arts.org.uk

## CLIMBING

*Pros:* Good for coordination, discipline, cooperation and physical confidence.

*Cons:* Can lead to a dangerous taste for mountains.

*Age:* From eight upwards at climbing walls. Many outdoor clubs do not accept under-sixteens, or even under-eighteens; some do if parents are climbers.

*Cost:* Low. Climbing walls all over the country.

**British Mountaineering Council** – provides information about local climbing walls and outdoor groups. Tel: 0870 010 4878. www.thebmc.co.uk

## COMBINED CADET FORCE

*Pros:* Weekends and training camps are very popular; once past the introductory stage, cadets can learn gliding, powerboating, scuba diving and other thrills.

*Cons:* Military style may not suit all.

*Age:* From thirteen (Year 9 at school) for CCF; from 12 for army, navy, but 13 for air cadets. Disabled welcome.

*Cost:* Low. Weekly meetings may be £1–2; a week's camp less than £100.

**Combined Cadet Force** is based in 245 schools, only 50 of which are state schools. Some will take candidates from neighbouring schools. There are now Outreach attempts to involve more disadvantaged young people. www.mod.uk

**Individual forces** – army, navy, air – now take cadets. Units are listed in local telephone directories or www.armycadets.com, www.sea-cadets.org and www.aircadets.org will provide information on nearest units.

## CREATIVE WRITING

*Pros:* Develops imagination, vocabulary and love of literature.

*Cons:* Might make children think they can earn a living as a writer.

*Cost:* Negligible.

**Achuka** – a children's book site. www.achuka.co.uk

**Book Trust** – Tel: 020 8516 2977. www.booktrust.org.uk

**Federation of Children's Book Groups** – Tel: 0113 258 8910. www.fcbc.org.uk

***Young Writer*** – magazine published three times a year; has competitions linked to World Book Day and National Poetry Day. Tel: 01544 318901. www.mystworld.com/youngwriter

## CRICKET

*Pros:* Players look nice in whites; girls now encouraged; good for fitness and sports scholarships; practice in parks.

*Cons:* Fewer cricket grounds these days (and players don't often wear whites).

*Age:* From five upwards children can play Kwik Cricket, with a soft ball; from twelve upwards they can play Inter Cricket, still with a softish ball.

*Cost:* Low after initial outlay on kit.

**England and Wales Cricket Board** – Tel: 020 7432 1200. www.Ecb.co.uk

**Kwik Cricket Action Line** – Tel: 0800 214 314. www.Ecb.co.uk

**National Cricket Academy** – based at Loughborough University, for university age students. Tel: 01509 222224. www.lboro.ac.uk

## CUBS & SCOUTS

*Pros:* Social; can go on good expeditions; open to all, including disabled.

*Cons:* Can be too wild for quiet children; lots of racing around.

*Age:* Beavers from six; Cubs from eight; Scouts from ten.

*Cost:* Subscriptions around £20 a year, plus a little at each meeting.

**Scout Association** – Tel: 0845 3001818. www.scoutbase.org.uk

## CYCLING

*Pros:* Good for heart and lungs; suits those who don't like team games; low impact on joints compared to running, as bike supports weight.

*Cons:* Finding a cycle track.

*Age:* From seven upwards

**British Cycling** – runs the off-road Go-ride programme for under-eighteens of all standards. Tel: 0870 871 2000. www.bcf.uk.com or www.go-ride.org.uk

## DANCE, GENERAL

**Council for Dance Education and Training** – offers information about specialist schools and colleges. Tel: 020 7247 4030. www.cdet.org.uk

**Foundation for Community Dance** – offers information about courses in all kinds of dance. Tel: 0116 251 0516. www.communitydance.org.uk

## DUKE OF EDINBURGH'S AWARD SCHEME

*Pros:* Great fun; demanding; opportunity to meet people; looks good on CV. Some awards are based on sporting challenges and expeditions, others on helping people.

*Cons:* Takes up quite a bit of time.

*Age:* From fourteen (or nearly fourteen) for bronze, fifteen for silver, sixteen for gold.

*Cost:* £10 for bronze award book; after that depends on which activities are chosen.

**Award information** – Tel: 01753 727400. www.theaward.org

## FENCING

*Pros:* Good for non-team players; mental and physical workout; teaches strategy, discipline, posture and hand–eye coordination.

*Cons:* Not to be practised at home.

*Age:* Usually from ten upwards, but Mini Musketeers, using foam swords and plastic masks, takes children from six up (introductory birthday parties arranged for sevens-plus).

*Cost:* £150 for a basic kit, plus lessons.

**British Fencing Association** – Tel: 0208 742 3032. www.british fencing.com

**Mini Musketeers** – Tel: 0795 0011581. www.minimusketeers.co.uk

## FISHING

*Pros:* Calming; skilful; country air.

*Cons:* Not very sociable.

*Age:* From ten upwards.

*Cost:* Taster days are free; courses £10–£30.

**Salmon & Trout Association** – runs junior fly-fishing courses. Tel: 020 7283 5838. www.salmon-trout.org

## FOOTBALL

*Pros:* Universally played now by both boys and girls; good for team spirit, fitness, coordination and cooperation.

*Cons:* Occasional injuries; can become all-consuming.

*Age:* Any, but most clubs start courses from four upwards.

Under-tens recommended to play seven-a-side. Each professional club is allowed to sign forty boys under ten, so scouts are out every weekend talent-spotting. Some clubs select girls for teams a year or two later.

*Cost:* Minimal; usually takes place in local parks. Clubs subsidise coaching. Expensive when you have to buy a season ticket to watch professional teams and over-priced strips.

**Football academies and training** – contact local professional clubs direct or via the FA (see below).

**Football Association** – has information about clubs and rules, and offers soccer parents online learning. It awards approved local clubs a symbol; runs courses at Lilleshall Sports Academy in Shropshire for 14–16-year-olds. Tel: 020 7745 4545. www.thefa.com

## GOLF

*Pros:* Fresh air; few injuries; good behaviour required.

*Cons:* Image problem (middle-aged); some clubs stuffy about correct clothes and discourage children.

*Age:* From five upwards.

*Cost:* Cheap at starter level (£3 per session), and equipment loaned free of charge. Moderately expensive thereafter for sets of clubs and club membership.

**Golf Foundation** – Dunlop Starter Centres teach basic skills, leading to the Junior Golf Passport, and from there to Tri-Golf Activator and Junior Golf Leader workshops. Tel: 01920 876200. www.Golf-foundation.org

## GYMNASTICS

*Pros:* Good for discipline, flexibility, teamwork.

*Cons:* Some coaches not safety aware; gymnasts can get bad backs later in life.

*Age:* From four upwards.

*Cost:* Around £16 a month, plus leotard, tracksuit, etc.

**British Gymnastics** – Tel: 0845 1297129. www.british-gymnastics.org

## HORSE RIDING

*Pros:* Fun and socially smart; children learn to care for an animal; good for active holidays.

*Cons:* Getting to the riding school; the pressure to own a pony; accidents (though back supports are now worn).

*Age:* From four upwards. Best to start before a child feels fear, but a very young child cannot control a horse.

*Cost:* High. Riding lessons from £20, though horse-mad older children can work in stables and get free rides. Cheaper if you live in the country and have friends with a pony.

**British Horse Society** – approves riding schools and gives info on riding holidays and holiday riding courses, usually for children of eight or over. Tel: 08701 202244. www.bhs.org.uk

**Pony Club** – runs gymkhanas and training sessions; has now instigated racing for 11–16s. Tel: 024 7669 8300. www.pony-club.org.uk

## KARTING

*Pros:* Appeals to would-be racing drivers – they all started this way; also good for hand–foot coordination, discipline and acting responsibly.

*Cons:* Awful 'neeoowww' noise; sedentary.

*Age:* From eight upwards, though there may also be a minimum height.

*Cost:* High. Most tracks provide an arrive-and-drive package (all equipment supplied) from £8 to £35 for a full training session.

**National Karting Association** – provides information on the 90-plus NKA-registered circuits, most of which operate junior fleets. Tel: 01206 322726. www.nationalkarting.co.uk

## LANGUAGES

*Pros:* Small children pick up second languages and good accents easily; from twelve onwards the brain discards connections that aren't being used. Good for general intelligence (solving complex problems), as well as job prospects and social ease.

*Cons:* Requires practice over dinner, on holiday or with specially hired au pair.

*Age:* The earlier the better.

*Cost:* BBC's *Muzzy* course is £143 for Level 1 (eight CDs); an au pair for a year would cost rather more, but would do the ironing.

**La Jolie Ronde** – runs 400 after-school French clubs for 5–11s. Tel: 01949 839715. www.lajolieronde.co.uk

**Local courses** – details available from libraries, embassies and specialist agencies, such as the Institut Français (tel: 020 7581 2701), the Goethe Institute (tel: 020 7411 3400) and the Italian Cultural Institute (tel: 020 7235 1461).

*Muzzy* – computer-based courses in a range of languages. Tel: 0800 138 3210. www.early-advantage.com or www.bbc.co.uk

## MAGIC

*Pros:* Good for hand–eye coordination and presentation skills; useful, too, for making a stir at parties.

*Cons:* Parents may have to watch tricks too often.

*Age:* Can join the Young Magicians Club aged ten.

*Cost:* Moderate. Pocket money suffices at first, but acquiring new tricks mounts up.

**Young Magicians Club** – for magicians under eighteen at all levels. Events and workshops mostly in London at the Centre for the Magic Arts. Tel: 020 7387 2222. www.theyoung magiciansclub.com

## MARTIAL ARTS

*Pros:* Good for children who like to work individually. Highly disciplined (suits both those who are disciplined and those who need to become so); teachers treated with respect; smart kit.

*Cons:* Male dominated, but changing – girls seem particularly to like karate. Some of the seven martial arts recognised by Sport England are not suitable for children as they are too aggressive, or involve the use of bows and sticks. Judo, karate and tae kwon-do are safe.

*Age:* From five, but only if a child is well coordinated and has a good attention span. Competitions from eight upwards.

*Cost:* Moderate in group classes. Uniforms cheap – the karate *gi* costs from £15.

**British Council for Chinese Martial Arts** – the governing body for karate, which involves use of the hands as well as the feet. Tel: 024 7639 4642. www.bccma.com

**British Judo Association** – judo involves more throwing and groundwork than karate. Recommended for the blind or visually impaired. Tel: 01949 839715. www.britishjudo.org.uk

**Tae Kwon-do Association of Great Britain** – combination of kicking and boxing; no throwing. Tel: 0800 052 5960. www.tagb.biz

## MATHS

*Pros:* Excellent for improving thinking skills, stretching the gifted and speeding up slower learners.

*Cons:* Not everyone's idea of fun; sedentary.

*Age:* As soon as children can count.

*Cost:* Kumon costs £41 a month, plus £15 joining fee.

**Kumon** – a Japanese system based on repetition, and taught in centres all over the UK. Teaches children speedy, accurate mental arithmetic at all levels (they also do English language). Requires daily practice. Tel: 0800 854714. www.kumon.co.uk

**UK Mathematics Trust** – runs competitions for 11–18-year-olds who fall in the top 35 per cent of ability. Entry via schools. www.ukmt.org.uk

## MODELLING

*Pros:* Good way for not-podgy, small-for-age children with attractive faces to earn (sometimes considerable) money. Provides passing fame; fun to try.

*Cons:* Missing school (officially should have permits from local authority). The child who gets hooked may be disappointed later, as prospects in adulthood are for taller, less quirky looks. Agencies say more boys carry on than girls. Most are London based.

*Age:* From birth. There are more jobs for babies than older children.

*Cost:* Moderate. Smart clothes needed for meetings, plus decent haircuts and good photos. Some agencies charge for listings. Travel expenses.

**Reputable agencies include:**

Bruce & Brown London Kids: 020 8968 5585

Childsplay: 020 8659 9860

Kids London: 020 7924 9595

Kids Plus: 020 7737 3901

Kidz: 0161 799 6788

Rascals: 020 8504 1111

Scallywags: 020 8553 9999

Elizabeth Smith: 020 8863 2331

Truly Scrumptious: 020 8888 4204

Tuesday's Child: 01625 612 244

***Contacts***, published by Spotlight (*see* **Acting**)

## MUSIC

*Pros:* Learning an instrument is good practice in listening, interpreting and appreciating music. Depending on whether it is a solo or orchestral instrument, it suits those who like to play alone or in company. Reaching Grade 8 and taking a diploma means you can teach.

*Cons:* Practising.

*Age:* From two upwards, using the Suzuki and Yamaha methods on a range of instruments. Other teachers prefer to start children at seven-plus, when less adult input is required.

*Cost:* High because of lessons and the need to hire or buy instruments, many of which cost more than £1000.

**Associated Board of the Royal Schools of Music** – offers advice for parents on choosing instruments, specialist schools, conservatories and youth orchestras. Tel: 020 7636 5400. www.abrsm.org

**British Suzuki Institute** – Tel: 01582 832424. www.british suzuki.com

**Centre for Young Musicians** – based at Morley College in London; weekend and holiday courses for all levels and all types of music, from classical to rock and jazz. Tel: 020 7928 3844. www.cymlondon.demon.co.uk

**Incorporated Society of Musicians** – provides information about teachers all over the country. Tel: 020 7629 4413. www.ism.org

*Music Education Yearbook* – listings of schools, including Chetham's, the Menuhin and the Purcell for the musically gifted.

**Yamaha Music Schools** – Tel: 020 7629 4413. www.yamaha-europe.com

## NETBALL

*Pros:* Good for those who aren't very athletic or are fearful.

*Cons:* Girly image; not many boys play, though teachers are trying to encourage them into the game.

*Cost:* Low.

**All England Netball Association** – organises junior versions of the game: First Step for 7–9s and High Five Netball for 9–11s are both played in mixed teams. Tel: 01462 442344. www.englandnetball.co.uk

## PUPPETRY

*Pros:* Good for entertaining and earning money; creative, and encourages crafts, such as making sets and props.

*Cons:* No fitness element; can be solitary.

*Age:* From seven or eight.

*Cost:* Can be considerable to buy good puppets, create a theatre and sets, etc.

**Puppeteers UK** – brings together the British Puppet and Model Theatre Guild (good for puppetry news), the Punch and Judy Fellowship and the Puppet Centre Trust, a support and reference organisation. Tel: 01869 245 793. www.puppeteers UK.com; www.punchandjudy.com; www.puppetcentre.com

## RADIO/TELEVISION PRESENTING

*Pros:* Glamorous; friends will be jealous.

*Cons:* Lose friends.

*Age:* Whenever confident enough.

*Cost:* Nil unless preparing a tape or show reel.

**For Radio:** BBC's Big Toe show has children on every day and a Reporters Club. Tel: 08700 100 700. The Big Toe Radio Show, BBC Broadcasting House, London W1A 1AA.

**For TV:** BBC Talent Scheme. Various schemes to encourage children, including one for young explorers 11–15. Hotline: 08700 106 060. www.bbc.co.uk/talent

Blast. Workshops, events opportunities for under 19s. www.bbc.co.uk/blast

Newsround, Children can apply to be 'press packers' on this CBBC programme.

**For tickets to favourite shows write to:** (name of show), BBC Television Centre, Wood Lane, London W12 7RJ. Many game shows take audiences from contestants' schools, not from members of the public.

## ROWING

*Pros:* Said to use more muscles than any other sport and doesn't cause many injuries.

*Cons:* Getting up early to practise.

*Age:* Clubs welcome children from nine upwards, rowing on canals and lakes as well as rivers. Children must be able to swim.

*Cost:* Club membership.

**Amateur Rowing Association** – Tel: 020 8237 6700. www.ara-rowing.org

# RUGBY

*Pros:* Great team spirit; the ultimate contact sport; wallow in mud; macho (although girls now play).

*Cons:* Broken noses and other injuries.

*Age:* From eleven upwards.

*Cost:* Minimal, though Rugby Union has strong private school links.

**British Amateur Rugby League Association** – Tel: 01484 549131. www.barla.org.uk

**Rugby Football League** – Tel: 0113 232 9111. www.rfl.uk

**Rugby Football Union** – Tel: 020 8892 8161. www.rfu.com

# SAILING

*Pros:* Good sport for the solitary; teaches fitness, organisation and quick thinking; good for jobs later as crew.

*Cons:* Need access to boats.

*Age:* From eight upwards. Need stamina and strength and to be able to swim.

*Cost:* Moderate. One instructor can teach only six students at a time, and courses last for days or weeks. Owning your own boat is not cheap.

**Association of Sea Training Organisations** – represents sail training schemes, often on classic vessels, for beginners and others. Has a small bursary scheme to help young people. Tel: 02392 364875. www.asto.org.uk

**Royal Yachting Association** – Tel: 0123 8060 4100. www.rya.org.uk

# SCHOLARSHIPS

*Pros:* Provides considerable discounts on independent school fees.

*Cons:* May make children feel under pressure.

*Age:* 11+, 13+ and sixth form.

*Cost:* Schools offer up to 50% of fees; in cases of hardship there may be bursaries to cover the rest of the fees.

***Independent Schools Yearbook***, published by A & C Black – full listings of scholarships of all kinds – music, sports, art, drama, academic plus odd-ball ones like riding.

# SHOOTING

*Pros:* Great days out in the country; a safe approach for those who fantasise about guns; conservation messages.

*Cons:* Not politically correct.

*Age:* From eleven upwards.

*Cost:* Only £10 a day, but the child has to be driven to a sporting estate.

**British Association for Shooting and Conservation** – runs a Young Guns programme for under-eighteens. Tel: 01244 573030. www.basc.org.uk

# SINGING

*Pros:* Social asset; good for general musicality; choirs are sociable, and delightful for parents. The Choir Schools Association represents forty-four schools, which together take 1000 singers, of whom just under a quarter are girls. It claims that being a chorister is 'the best educational bargain around'. Training a boy's voice before it breaks will help him to have a good voice later.

*Cons:* Belonging to a choir demands commitment to getting up early and working weekends and holidays. Girls are welcome in some, but still not all, choir schools; there are more places for them in the voluntary choirs runs by cathedrals and parish churches.

*Age:* From seven to thirteen (when most boys' voices break), to eighteen for girls. (Boys can resume when their voices have settled down).

*Cost:* Some choirs are free; specialist singing teachers can be expensive.

**Choir Schools Association** – choir schools prefer raw material (untrained children who can hold a tune and are eager) as they have their own styles of training. Tel: 01359 221333. www.choirsschools.org.uk

**Incorporated Society of Musicians** – for information on singing teachers. Tel: 020 7629 4413. www.ism.org

## SKATING

*Pros:* Good for balance, control and general fitness; enjoyable to watch; ice hockey is very fast.

*Cons:* Ice rinks are scarce and you can't practise at home. The more advanced the child, the earlier it means getting up in the morning for training and competitions. Rinks are cold places to hang around.

*Age:* From five for skating. The most junior ice hockey league is for under-tens.

*Cost:* Basic level courses in Skate UK grades 1–10 and gold, silver and bronze are cheap. Individual tuition for the more advanced taking NISA tests in figure-skating or dance gets pricey.

**English Ice Hockey Association** – has details of clubs. www.eiha.co.uk

**National Ice Skating Association** – Tel: 0115 9888060. www.ice skating.org.uk

## SKIING

*Pros:* Exciting; good for fitness; jobs for students in gap years.

*Cons:* Breakages (of banks and legs); addictive.

*Age:* The younger the better, as not inhibited by fear.

*Cost:* Skiing holidays cost a lot, even when organised by a school. Dry ski slopes are not much of a substitute.

**Snowsport England** – for information on children's snowsports. Tel: 0121 501 2314. www.snowsportgb.com or www.snow sportengland.org.uk

## SNOOKER

*Pros:* Cool; good for concentration.

*Cons:* Indoors; not much exercise.

*Age:* Many top players have started when they can barely see the tabletop.

*Cost:* Low.

**English Association for Snooker and Billiards** – has details about 2500 clubs and coaching across the country. Tel: 07947 782275. www.easb.co.uk

**World Snooker** – the official body for snooker and billiards; also gives details of other associations. www.worldsnooker.com

## SPORT, GENERAL

**Sport England** – provides general information and contacts for a wide selection of sports. Tel: 020 7273 1500. www.sport england.org.

**Sportscoach** – a relatively new Saturday-school venture from Stagecoach, which introduces children aged 6–16 of all abilities to a wide range of sports. Tel: 0800 0853542. www.sportscoachschools.co.uk

## SQUASH

*Pros:* Hard and fast; very good for fitness and mental alertness.

*Cons:* A bit scary; can be exhausting; considered mostly for grown-ups.

*Age:* As soon as they're old enough to pick up a racket; can build up coordination with 'mini-squash', using special rackets and soft balls.

*Cost:* Low (rackets, trainers and court hire).

**Squash England (National Squash Centre)** – Tel: 0161 231 4499. www.squashplayer.co.uk or www.minisquash.com

## SWIMMING

*Pros:* Available everywhere; good cardiovascular exercise, with minimal injuries; develop big shoulders.

*Cons:* All that chlorine; maybe don't want big shoulders; can't practise at home.

*Age:* Start as young as possible to get used to the water. FUNdamental courses teach the four basic strokes to girls aged 5–8 and boys aged 6–9. Serious training from age twelve.

*Cost:* Minimal – goggles and club membership fees.

**Amateur Swimming Association** – the governing body for swimming, diving, water polo, open water and synchronised swimming. Supports 1600 affiliated clubs. Tel: 01509 618700. www.britishswimming.org

## TABLE TENNIS

*Pros:* Can have a fold-up table at home.
*Cons:* Usually indoors.
*Age:* Need to be able to see over the table.
*Cost:* Tables cost around £300.
**English Table Tennis Association** – Tel: 01424 722525. www.etta.co.uk

## TENNIS

*Pros:* Outdoor exercise; good for fitness and mental skills; socially useful.
*Cons:* Highly competitive because high rewards for top players.
*Age:* From four upwards. Mini tennis programmes for 4–10s use smaller courts and rackets, and less bouncy balls.
*Cost:* Group lessons cheap. Private coaching from £20.
**Lawn Tennis Association** – has information on clubs with junior programmes, First Serve holiday camps and competitions, and the four LTA Performance Academies for promising players in Bath, Leeds, Loughborough and Welwyn. Tel: 020 7381 7000. www.lta.org.uk

## WOODCRAFT FOLK

*Pros:* Good camping outings and social activities for the environmentally concerned.
*Cons:* Having to explain constantly that the organisation has nothing to do with hugging trees or whittling wood.
*Age:* The youngest group is for under sixes; goes up to young adults.
*Cost:* Low: 50p – £1 a week; no membership fee for children
**Woodcraft Folk** – Tel: 020 8672 6031. www.woodcraft.org.uk

# USEFUL ADDRESSES

**Cassandra Jardine** has a website www.cassandrajardine.com and can be emailed at cassandrajardine@gmail.com

**Noël Janis-Norton** and her staff of learning and behaviour specialists teach the 'Calmer, Easier, Happier Parenting' methods through workshops and classes at the New Learning Centre (NLC) and in schools, as well as through private sessions and telephone consultations. Their senior lecturers also give seminars for teachers and other youth professionals in many UK cities on topics such as:

- Improving Classroom Behaviour
- Helping the Atypical Learner to Thrive, Not Just Survive
- Preventing and Reducing Bullying
- Involving Parents as Partners in Education
- Raising Standards Through Effective Differentiation

In addition, the NLC also produces and sells a range of audio tapes and booklets on many different aspects of parenting and teaching. The classes for children, which are held during holidays and half-terms, teach basic academic skills, learning strategies, social skills and positive behaviour and attitudes.

The NLC's 'Time Out Programme' is a temporary alternative to mainstream schooling for children with acute problems. It is a demonstration school, where parents and educators come to observe and learn about the NLC's unique methods by seeing them in action. Anyone is welcome to book an appointment to observe (after having listened to one of the audio tapes, which serves as an introduction to the methods).

**The New Learning Centre**
211 Sumatra Road
London NW6 1PF
Tel: 020 7794 0321
Fax: 020 7431 8600
E-mail: tnlc@dial.pipex.com
Website: www.tnlc.info

**Luke Scott** runs summer workshops for fathers and sons. He also leads groups of parents who want to improve their skills. Despite the organisation's name, many of the courses and materials on offer are equally relevant to women and girls.

**Boys to Men**
E-mail: lukescott@boystomen.co.uk
Website: www.boystomen.co.uk

# INDEX